Fallen Angels

One Man's True Encounters with Evil

by
Tim Maddocks

TEACH Services, Inc.
P U B L I S H I N G
www.TEACHServices.com • (800) 367-1844

Copyright © 2025 Tim Maddocks
Copyright © 2025 TEACH Services, Inc.
Published in Calhoun, Georgia, USA
ISBN-13: 978-1-4796-1932-0 (Paperback)
ISBN-13: 978-1-4796-1933-7 (ePub)
Library of Congress Control Number: 2025911978

TEACH Services, Inc.
P U B L I S H I N G
www.TEACHServices.com • (800) 367-1844

PUBLISHER'S FOREWORD:
The Western Blindspot

Western minds dismiss what they cannot measure—and demons count on it. This demon possession book shatters the materialistic worldview that keeps millions enslaved to invisible forces. After four decades, Tim Maddocks continues documenting supernatural evidence that defies scientific explanation: stones that speak, objects that reappear after being discarded, superhuman strength in possessed teenagers, and lightning striking on command. These aren't primitive superstitions—they're spiritual laws crossing over into the physical world.

The Holy Spirit reveals what Western education conceals: demons exploit our rational blindness. While we medicate anxiety, they feed on emotional wounds. While we blame genetics for addictions, they maintain generational strongholds. While we pursue therapy for relationship problems, they whisper lies we mistake for our own thoughts. Tim's exorcism accounts expose their hidden strategies: how they use entertainment as entry points, sometimes disguise themselves as mental illness, and even counterfeit spiritual gifts in churches.

But knowledge brings power. Read this book, and you'll learn to recognize spiritual evidence your culture trained you to ignore—sudden personality changes, objects linked to apparently unrelated problems, supernatural timing of "accidents," and physical symptoms that defy medical explanation. More importantly, you'll discover how to wield Christ's authority against forces operating with increasing aggressiveness in Western societies, yet remain unnoticed even by many Christians.

The demons manifesting violently in these pages prove one thing: their hidden kingdom thrives on ignorance. Every reader who gains spiritual sight threatens their invisible empire. Will you remain blindfolded by Western materialism, or will you see what's really happening around you?

Michael W. Brazington

TABLE OF CONTENTS

PUBLISHER'S FOREWORD: The Western Blindspot iii

SECTION ONE:
AWAKENING TO THE SPIRITUAL REALM: *Learning Basic Deliverance*... 9

INTRODUCTION: When Darkness First Attacked 11

The First Attack of Darkness

Walking onto Enemy Ground

Sensing the Unseen: The Hospital Revelation

To the Front Lines!

CHAPTER 1: First Encounters 17

From Fury to Empty Eyes: The Zombie Boy

The Eyes That Burned

SECTION TWO:
THE RULES OF SPIRITUAL WARFARE: *How Spirits Gain Legal Rights*.. 23

CHAPTER 2: The Power of Objects and Places.............................. 25

The Talking Stone

Satan Sent Lightning

Build Us a House and We Will Leave

Spiritual Strongholds

CHAPTER 3: Open Doors 35

 The Palm Reader   ·

 I Made a Pact with a Legion of Demons

CHAPTER 4: Emotional Gateways 41

 Cloaked with a Grey Shadow

 The Demon of Self-Pity

 A Demon of Anger

SECTION THREE:
SATANIC DECEPTION: *Recognizing Demonic Tricks* 51

CHAPTER 5: Is It Medical or Spiritual? 53

 Demons Can Dance

 Demonic Malaria

 Epilepsy or Demons

CHAPTER 6: False Identities 63

 Lucifer is the Son of God!

 My Name is Lucifer

 Smoked Baby Talks

CHAPTER 7: Counterfeit Gifts 71

 Speaking in Tongues

 Her Writing Hand

 The Girl with Sapphire Eyes

 The Blood-Curdling Scream

SECTION FOUR:
DEEPENING THE MINISTRY: *Advanced Lessons* 81

CHAPTER 8: Healing Inner Wounds 83

 Burn The Oxcart

 Coming Out of Deep Depression

 Caterpillars in the Brain

 Srey Day's Abandonment & Anger

CHAPTER 9: Special Cases 93

    My Boy Wakes Up Screaming Every Night

    Multiple Reasons for Harassment

    Typhoid, Not Demons

CHAPTER 10: The Cost of Ministry 101

    Sexual Temptation: A Satanic Strategy

    Attacked Personally

    Don't Read That Book!

SECTION FIVE:

MATURE UNDERSTANDING: *Understanding Tragic Outcomes*....113

CHAPTER 11: When Deliverance Doesn't Come 115

    Zero Day

    Black Magic Took His Life

    Demons Defile Our Character

    The Shocking Scope of Demonic Influence

    The Battle Is Ours Through Christ

    When We Fail, We're Not Forgotten

    Our Call to Victory

EPILOGUE: 137

SECTION ONE:

AWAKENING TO THE SPIRITUAL REALM:
Learning Basic Deliverance

INTRODUCTION:
When Darkness First Attacked

The First Attack of Darkness

"Be on your guard and stay awake. Your enemy, the devil, is like a roaring lion, sneaking around to find someone to attack" (1 Peter 5:8, CEV).

I first felt a demon's sneaking attack when I was twelve. I was relaxing on the couch watching a Disney movie when it began—a whispering in my mind that made my stomach tighten. The words "I hate God" began repeating over and over in my head. Confusion washed over me because I knew this was a lie. I loved God and was a baptized member of His church, but the words "I hate God" seemed to be coming from my own mind.

In that moment of inner turmoil, a remarkable clarity cut through the confusion. The Holy Spirit illuminated a truth that would forever change my understanding of spiritual warfare: this voice, though it mimicked my internal voice, was not my own. An evil spirit was attempting to plant thoughts of blasphemy in my mind.

More surprising was the connection the Holy Spirit helped my young mind make. This seemingly harmless entertainment contained hidden themes that opened a dark door. This first encounter with demonic influence raised compelling questions: How many people mistake demonic influence for their own thoughts? What seemingly innocent activities open doors to darkness? If I hadn't recognized this external influence, would I have eventually believed these thoughts were my own, allowing them to create distance between me and my Creator? What happens to people who invite evil spirits into their lives? In **Chapter 1**, I begin describing some of those people and the destruction and trauma demons inflict on their bodies and minds.

Walking onto Enemy Ground

Two years later, I experienced a stronger attack, which confirmed the reality of the invisible war surrounding us. At fourteen, my passion for exploring God's creation had grown into a deep fascination with Australian wildlife. Books about native animals easily drew me in. Each new animal gave me a glimpse into the creative mind of God Himself.

One afternoon, while walking home from school through the busy streets of Perth, Australia, I was thrilled to see multicolored books spilling out of a new bookstore. The sidewalk displays beckoned me inside, where I expected to find the nature section. However, a few steps into the store, my body responded like I had just walked into a poisoned cloud. A wave of nausea rolled into my body, and my muscles felt weak.

What's happening to me? Why the almost-instant change in well-being?

Alarmed and confused, my eyes focused carefully around the store. What I saw were books about witchcraft, new age practices, spirit channeling, crystal healing, tarot reading, and other occult topics. I turned around and almost ran out of the shop.

As soon as I left, the ill feelings left me. The contrast between the heaviness inside the store and the normalcy outside was so stark that I had to process what had just happened. The spiritual realm had manifested in physical symptoms. My reaction was as real as an allergic response. My body had recognized the danger before my conscious mind could process it. As a Christian who loved Jesus, I had been instantly identified as an intruder in that territory dedicated to darkness. I had stepped into a Satanic stronghold, and the evil spirits wasted no time in attacking me to let me know I was not welcome.

What would happen to someone without Christ's protection who wandered into such a place? How might the entities there attach themselves to the unsuspecting? And what would it take to set such a person free?

These questions would begin to find real answers 8 years later, when I was 22, working with a teenager named Semo, whom I talk about in Chapter 1.

Sensing the Unseen: The Hospital Revelation

A third encounter happened at the unexpected setting of Royal Perth Hospital. My mother worked on the psychiatric ward, and I often waited there after school until her shift ended. While waiting, I watched many people coming and going. One afternoon, something peculiar began happening. Certain patients walking through the area created a distinct discomfort in me.

The feeling of unease had nothing to do with their physical appearance. The sensation was inconsistent and puzzling. Some patients triggered it strongly, while others produced no reaction at all. The feeling wasn't fear exactly, but more like recognition. A part of me could detect something invisible surrounding these individuals. Curious about this phenomenon, I began studying the people more intentionally, focusing on what might be causing the difference in my reactions. Was it something in their expressions? Their manner of walking? Nothing visible explained the pattern.

Lord, what am I sensing? I prayed silently, opening my mind to divine guidance.

The answer came with startling clarity: I was detecting the presence of evil spirits. Not all psychiatric patients triggered this response—only those whose mental conditions had a demonic component. At just fourteen years old, God began granting me a spiritual sensitivity that would later become crucial to my ministry.[1]

I shared my experience with my mother that evening, hoping for confirmation.

"It's just chemical imbalances in their brains," she explained, her voice gentle but dismissive.

I wanted to accept her medical explanation. It aligned with everything modern society told me about mental illness. Yet my experience testified to another factor. Now in my sixties, I've had forty years of experience with evil spirits. I've prayed with people exhibiting behaviors that baffled medical professionals. I've witnessed Jesus free people from tormenting spirits,

---

1   This is called "discerning of spirits" in 1 Corinthians 12:10. I give all glory to God. I want to emphasize here that *everyone* who pursues growing faith in Jesus will receive the Holy Spirit. "Seek and you will find," Jesus said (Luke 11:9). The Holy Spirit gives different gifts to different people (according to His will not always our will), but our Heavenly Father offers this to anyone who will forsake his sins and trust in Jesus with his or her whole heart just as Chapter 5 shows in *Demons Can Dance*.

restoring them to mental clarity and peace. That teenage insight in a hospital lobby wasn't imagination—it was preparation for a calling I couldn't yet comprehend.

> *That teenage insight in a hospital lobby wasn't imagination— it was preparation for a calling I couldn't yet comprehend.*

This raises uncomfortable questions for our modern understanding of mental health and emotional problems: Could some patients in psychiatric facilities be there because of demonic influence rather than merely chemical imbalances? What would happen if medical professionals recognized spiritual causes alongside physical ones? How many might find freedom through spiritual intervention alongside Christian medical care? My encounters in **Chapter 4:** *Emotional Gateways* and **Chapter 5:** *Is It Medical or Spiritual?* show the intersection between emotional and physical problems and evil spirits.

To the Front Lines!

Every disciple of Christ is called to shine as light in the world. Jesus himself commanded his disciples in Matthew 10:7-8: "As you go, preach, saying, 'The kingdom of heaven is at hand.' Heal the sick, cleanse the lepers, raise the dead, *cast out demons*. Freely you have received, freely give." This command is for today because as the following chapters testify, Satan is still holding people captive, and Jesus is still casting out demons by His Spirit working in people who answer His call.

When the Apostle Paul encountered Jesus on the Damascus road, he received the same commission we are called to: "I send you to open their eyes, and to turn them from darkness to light, and from the power of Satan unto God, that they may receive forgiveness of sins, and inheritance among them which are sanctified by faith that is in me" (Acts 26:18).

Who will step into the authority Jesus gives to set captives free? Who will look beyond material explanations our culture offers for suffering and learn to discern the hidden causes? As you journey with me through these true encounters with demons, my prayer is that you'll not only learn to protect yourself but also discover how to partner with Jesus in liberating others from

Satan's power. The frontlines of this spiritual war run through our homes, schools, workplaces, churches, and hospitals. Are you ready to see the battle that rages around us?

Tim Maddocks

June 2025

Siem Reap, Cambodia

CHAPTER 1:
First Encounters

From Fury to Empty Eyes: The Zombie Boy

The afternoon sun beat down on the sports field as Semo played with his classmates. Semo was a pastor's son who enjoyed being on the sports field. He was athletic and liked by his peers, but today, when he realized his team had lost, something frightening happened.

Semo's friendly demeanor vanished. His face contorted with rage. His classmates braced for an explosive outburst, but then Semo's expression emptied completely. His body stiffened. His arms extended straight out before him like a sleepwalker from a horror film. His eyes, moments ago flashing with anger, now stared vacantly ahead like a zombie. He seemed to be seeing nothing, recognizing no one.

A terrified student sprinted toward the staff housing where my wife, Wendy, served as the school nurse. "Come quick! Something's wrong with Semo!"

This wasn't the first time. Whenever these episodes occurred, Wendy would send me to guide Semo home. I would find him frozen in this trance-like state, arms outstretched, completely unresponsive to his name or any questions. I would physically position his rigid body in the direction of our house and walk alongside him, speaking gentle reassurances that he showed no sign of hearing. Once inside our home, I would gently stroke Semo's arm, which seemed to calm him and lull him to sleep. When he awoke later, he had no memory of the episode.

What was happening to this young man? What triggered the transformation from normal teenager to this robotic state?

During one episode, curiosity prompted me to test Semo's strength in this zombie state. Placing my hands on just one of his arms, I gradually shifted my weight until I was suspended completely off the ground. His arm remained perfectly horizontal, supporting my entire 132 pounds (60 kg) without trembling. No teenage boy possessed such unnatural strength and stability. Something I did not know how to explain was happening to Semo's body during these strange experiences, which he could not later recall.

Wendy, concerned that Semo might have a neurological condition, took him to a French doctor working with Médecins Sans Frontières. After listening to descriptions of the episodes, the doctor concluded that Semo was overtaxing his brain with studies.

> *I wanted to believe the doctor, but his diagnosis didn't seem like a reasonable explanation for the supernatural strength Semo had in his trance states.*

"He needs rest," the doctor prescribed confidently. "His mind is simply shutting down from too much pressure."

I wanted to believe the doctor, but his diagnosis didn't seem like a reasonable explanation for the supernatural strength Semo had in his trance states. As Semo's episodes became more frequent and disruptive, an uncomfortable conviction grew in my mind. Could Semo be experiencing demon possession? The possibility both frightened and challenged me. At twenty-two years old, I had no formal training in this area, so how could I possibly confront such a situation?

This entire experience challenged me. I had read Bible stories about demon possession, but this was the first time I saw something this close and personal. I thought back to my experiences as a teenager watching psychiatric patients while I waited for my mom to get off work at the hospital. The Holy Spirit had convicted me back then that evil spirits were real and their activity was sometimes the cause of strange behavior. As a Christian, I believed demons were real. However, believing something is real and experiencing it up close are two different things. This situation was far more confrontational than I was comfortable with.

The idea of commanding an unseen demon to leave did not come naturally to me. I was raised in a secular Western environment where demons are typically portrayed as fictional characters, like red dragons with pitchforks.

I thought back to my mother's medical explanation for the odd behavior of the psychiatric patients, and I began to understand why a strictly medical explanation for demonic activity could be appealing. The world would be a less frightening place if evil spirits did not exist. It's easier to feel in control when we reduce the universe to physical laws that we can understand and control.

I wanted to believe the doctor when he said that Semo's experiences would disappear if he rested. I did not want to look foolish for acting on my belief in demons. I explored the idea that maybe Semo's superhuman strength could be some kind of medical condition. However, a medical explanation could not account for the growing pattern we began to observe.

Semo's episodes increasingly coincided with Friday evenings when students gathered to welcome the Sabbath. During worship times, he would enter his trance-like state then vocalize his disapproval of the sacred activities.

What medical condition specifically targets times of worship? I wondered.

I confided my suspicions to Vic, the school principal. "I think we might be dealing with something supernatural," I said.

Vic nodded gravely. "I've been thinking the same thing."

We decided to conduct a deliverance prayer for Semo. Beforehand, we studied the New Testament to understand how Jesus performed deliverance. Uncertainty gnawed at me. What if nothing happened? What if something worse occurred? I had no theological training for this, only the examples in Scripture where Jesus and His disciples confronted demonic forces. I realized at some point I had to make a choice to act on my belief in the Bible even in my uncertainty.

Would that be enough?

On Friday evening, we gathered in the boys' dormitory office. Semo sat before us, once again in his trance-like state. Drawing courage from the New Testament accounts, Vic and I began to pray.

"In the name of Jesus Christ," I commanded, my voice stronger than I felt, "evil spirit, come out of him!"

Unlike many later encounters where demons would fight violently against eviction, this spirit departed at once. Semo emerged from his trance immediately. From then on, the strange manifestations stopped. Semo returned to being a normal teenager—no more zombie-like trances, no more supernatural strength, no more disruptions during Sabbath hours.

This experience forced me to confront uncomfortable realities about spiritual warfare. The pattern of Semo's manifestations revealed two significant insights: anger often preceded the onset of his episodes, and the evil spirit targeted sacred Sabbath hours. Satan loves to use sin—in this case, anger—as an entry point into human lives, and he harbors special hatred for holy times when God's people draw near to their Savior.

What doors might we unknowingly open through unchecked emotions? How many "mental breakdowns" or "personality disorders" might actually have spiritual components that modern medicine isn't equipped to diagnose? And how might our understanding of human behavior change if we acknowledged the reality of spiritual influences—both divine and demonic?

These questions would multiply as my encounters with demons continued over the next 40 years, but so would the answers.

The Eyes That Burned

The fluorescent lights of the library hummed quietly as students bent over their textbooks during evening study period. As supervisor, I moved between tables, ensuring the atmosphere remained conducive to learning. Most evenings passed without incident, but tonight would prove dramatically different.

Ryan, a powerfully built young man from the Solomon Islands, had come to Fiji's Fulton Seventh-day Adventist College to further his education. Tonight, Ryan was becoming increasingly disruptive. He was disrupting those trying to concentrate. After gentle reminders failed to subdue Ryan, I gave him a verbal warning.

"Ryan, you need to respect the other students who are trying to study. Please stop being disruptive."

The words had barely left my mouth when Ryan exploded from his chair. Before I could react, his hand flew forward. He clamped his hand around my throat, using his momentum to force me onto the librarian's desk, pinning me as his grip tightened.

Looking up into his face, I froze. Ryan's eyes had transformed. What should have been normal human eyes now appeared to glow with an internal fire. Rivulets of fire seemed to radiate outward from his pupils, creating an effect I'd only seen in horror movie advertisements.

In that moment, I knew I wasn't facing merely an angry student. Something supernatural had taken control.

"I could crush you," Ryan snarled.

Someone said something about reporting Ryan to the principal. The mention of authority seemed to penetrate whatever had overtaken him. His grip loosened, and he backed away, storming out of the library without another word.

I stood there, shaken by what I had witnessed in Ryan's eyes even more than the physical assault. What had I just encountered? At that point in my spiritual journey, I lacked the knowledge that Ryan could have been set free. If properly rebuked in Jesus' name, the evil spirit controlling him would have been forced to release its grip and depart.

Instead, Ryan remained under demonic influence, and the consequences proved devastating. Weeks later, female students came forward with terrifying reports: they had witnessed Ryan walking through the solid walls of their dormitory rooms at night, holding some kind of fetish object in his hands. The supernatural manifestations had escalated.

Ryan was expelled and returned to the Solomon Islands without completing his education, still captive to the demonic power that controlled him.

What had opened the door to such extreme demonic activity in Ryan's life? Though I couldn't know with certainty, his background offered clues. While the Solomon Islands had largely embraced Christianity by this time, many people still worshiped evil spirits as their ancestors had for generations.

In many animistic cultures, spiritual power passes through bloodlines, with spirit priests or witch doctors receiving supernatural abilities from the entities that enslave them. These malevolent spirits often claim generational rights, frequently targeting firstborn children to continue their hold on families.

Had Ryan been caught in such a generational claim? Was he perhaps the victim of spirits that had attached themselves to his family line through ceremonies or pacts made by ancestors?

The reality I was beginning to understand is that black magic is not mere superstition—it represents actual supernatural power granted by spirits to their human servants. But these powers come at a catastrophic price: spiritual enslavement. Breaking free from the iron grip of such entities is impossible without divine intervention.

This encounter with Ryan raised profound questions that would shape my developing ministry: How many people carry generational spiritual bondage without realizing it? What happens when traditional spiritual practices collide with Christian faith? And most urgently—how can those trapped in such bondage find freedom through Jesus Christ?

The answers would unfold gradually through increasingly challenging confrontations with evil spirits.

SECTION TWO:

THE RULES OF SPIRITUAL WARFARE:
How Spirits Gain Legal Rights

CHAPTER 2:
The Power of Objects and Places

The Talking Stone

"Something terrible happened last night," Sreynich whispered, clearly shaken. She held out a small stone, her fingers trembling slightly. "This stone … it has something attached to it."

The previous day had been like any other Sunday—a group of our Bible students had gone sightseeing. While exploring the ancient ruins of Angkor Wat and its surrounding temples, Sreynich had picked up a piece of stone that had cracked off of a temple wall. Thinking it was fine-grained sandstone suitable for sharpening her knife, she had slipped it into her bag and brought it back to her dormitory room at the SALT Center.

What happened next would forever change her understanding of the spirit world.

"I laid the stone down near my bed last night," Sreynich continued, her voice shaking. "In the middle of the night, suddenly my roommate woke up. An angry male voice seemed to be coming from my bedside! 'I don't like being taken away from my temple!' it said."

Her roommate, also present, nodded confirmation. "Then something invisible grabbed Sreynich by the neck and shook her awake," she added. "I commanded whatever it was to leave in Jesus' name, and it released her. We felt something like wind rush out the window."

Looking at the innocuous-appearing stone in Sreynich's hand, I was reminded of the lesson I had taught just days earlier about spiritual strongholds—how even seemingly harmless objects can serve as anchors for demonic entities. I had shared Pastor Daniel Walter's experience from Borneo, where a convert to Christianity had discovered that a spiritually charged metal ring kept returning to his home even after being thrown away—until they burned it while claiming the blood of Jesus to break the demons' authority over it.

The Angkorian civilization had been deeply immersed in idol worship, constructing Angkor Wat and more than 400 other worship sites throughout Siem Reap province. These ancient acts of idol worship had granted evil spirits territorial rights—spirit strongholds that remained active centuries later. What appeared to be just a piece of stone to Sreynich was, in the spiritual realm, still claimed territory.

> *I discarded it in our outside bin, but a few days later, I found the exact same shirt folded neatly in my drawer!*

"What should I do?" Sreynich asked, clearly not wanting to spend another night with the haunted stone.

I gathered the students together, using this frightening experience as a teaching moment. "This is why we must be careful about what we bring into Christian spaces," I explained. "Even objects that seem harmless can have spiritual attachments."

We prayed together, asking God's forgiveness for inadvertently bringing a fragment of a spirit stronghold into a Christian dwelling. Then we built a small fire, and Sreynich threw the stone into the flames—a visible act of severing ties with the evil spirit that had accompanied it.

"From this point forward," I told the watching students, "that spirit has no authority to return. The blood of Jesus breaks its claim."

The incident with Sreynich's stone wasn't isolated. Years later, I shared this story with a group of students from Avondale College in Australia. One student, Amy Townsend, approached me afterward with her own unsettling experience.

"I bought a t-shirt from the markets in Siem Reap," Amy recounted. "It featured a Hindu god, although I didn't realize its religious significance then. I chose it because I thought it looked 'artsy.' After hearing your warning about objects from temples, I felt convicted to throw it away when I returned home to Perth. I discarded it in our outside bin, but a few days later, I found the exact same shirt folded neatly in my drawer! No one in my family had retrieved it. This time, I waited until the garbage truck arrived and made sure I watched it leave. After that, I never saw it again."

More recently, a volunteer teacher at our school received several scarves featuring Angkor Wat temple designs as a going-away gift. Despite hesitation about the printed images, she accepted them to avoid offending the giver. With the scarves in her luggage, she flew to Japan where she planned to prayer-walk the streets of Tokyo with a fellow volunteer. Immediately upon arrival, she fell mysteriously ill. This prevented her participation in the prayer walk and made it impossible to board her next flight.

During the night, her travel companion woke with a strong impression that the scarves needed to be disposed of. The next morning she shared this with her sick friend, who by now had decided to keep them as a gift for a close relative and was reluctant to part with them. The following day, the issue was raised again, and they decided to cut the scarves up and throw them away. As they destroyed the scarves, a distinct presence of the Holy Spirit filled the room, and the sick traveler began to recover immediately.

What connects these three experiences? The recognition that seemingly innocuous objects—a piece of stone, a decorative t-shirt, or tourist scarves—can serve as conduits for the influence of evil spirits when they're connected to idolatry or demonic worship.

Many people make the same mistake, believing that artistic representations or fragments have no spiritual significance. But in the unseen realm, these items remain claimed territory. Artifacts or replicas associated with idol worship should not be in a Christian's possession. Keeping such items in our homes, gardens, vehicles, or workplaces can grant demonic entities access to ourselves and our families.

The proper response isn't to sell such items, regardless of their monetary value. Selling or giving away spiritually compromised objects only transfers the problem to someone else. Instead, they should be destroyed completely, even if it means financial loss. Additionally, it's important to confess to God any unintentional invitation of demonic influence and ask that any spiritual agreements—made knowingly or unknowingly—be canceled by the blood of Jesus.

As we look around our homes and workplaces, what objects might we have innocently brought in that could be spiritual liabilities? What souvenirs, artwork, or decorative items might have connections to religious systems opposed to Christ? Sreynich's experience reminds us that spiritual warfare isn't just about dramatic confrontations—it's also about the subtle doorways we may unknowingly leave open.

Satan Sent Lightning

The spiritual battle intensified as I encountered a case that would demonstrate just how far demons will go to maintain control over their victims.

A woman named Roan sat before me in our simple clinic, her malnourished infant daughter cradled weakly in her arms. Through my translator, Danee, she shared her story—one that began with a mysterious dreadlock that had formed in her hair.

"It wasn't a normal matted patch," Roan explained, her eyes reflecting remembered fear. "It formed the perfect shape of a male human, with a head, arms, and legs. No matter how I tried to comb it out, it would return to the same shape within a day or two."

The appearance of this unnatural dreadlock had coincided with mounting health problems. Village elders had warned her never to cut it off, reinforcing their warning with stories of those who had tried.

"One woman cut her dreadlock and went blind for three days," Roan continued. "When she cut it again after it regrew, her house burned down that same day. She swore she would never cut it again, fearing something worse would happen."

Desperate for help, Roan had first sought assistance from a Buddhist monk. He advised her to let him perform a ceremonial cutting, which he did. She then carefully preserved the dreadlock, wrapping it in a new cloth. Though nothing catastrophic followed this ritual, her health continued to deteriorate. When she gave birth, her body produced no milk for her infant, forcing her to feed the baby starchy rice water that provided minimal nutrition.

Growing more desperate, Roan had stayed with a Kru Khmer—a traditional healer with spiritual powers. His treatments had been brutal. He gave her pounded chili juice to drink. This caused violent diarrhea, but the spirits did not leave. Then, he used burning incense sticks to drive out the spirits. "This gave me thirty-six small burns on my chest, abdomen, and thighs," she said. "The tropical humidity quickly infected the burns, further complicating my health issues." It was clear to her that the evil spirits remained.

"My baby daughter was thin and weak since her only nutrition came from the rice porridge water." Roan's case was desperate, but that's when she heard some news that was to change her life: "I heard about a kind foreign woman in a nearby village who was known for healing the sick." She explained. "I was afraid of what the Kru Khmer might do to me next, so I left his home and came to the foreigner's clinic."

My wife, Wendy, listened to Roan's story and was horrified to see the infected burn marks. Wendy treated Roan's infections and provided formula for her malnourished daughter, promising to continue the supply until the baby could survive on solid foods. But the root problem remained spiritual—no amount of medical intervention would address the demonic attachment that was destroying this woman's life.

Roy returned with the dreadlock. The battle was about to begin.

After explaining who Jesus is and His power over evil spirits, I made Roan an offer: "If you're willing to remove the waist charm you wear for protection against spirits, and if your husband brings the preserved dreadlock, we can burn them. I'll pray to the God of heaven to set you free from the demons causing your health problems."

Roan agreed, sending her husband Roy to retrieve the dreadlock from their village. Roy returned with the dreadlock. The battle was about to begin.

Listening to Roan made me realize how easy it is to view people's lives superficially, remaining oblivious to the spirit world's impact on their choices, words, and actions. Paul speaks of this in Ephesians 6:12: "For we wrestle not against flesh and blood, but against principalities, against powers, against the rulers of the darkness of this world, against spiritual wickedness in high places." This struggle against the 'rulers of darkness' is a reality in our daily lives. Sadly, most people only know to appease the spirits, or they attribute their struggles to bad luck, or they seek medical help for a problem that is actually spiritual. With Jesus in our lives and with the guidance of the Holy Spirit, we can take an offensive stance against these powers of darkness and experience true freedom in Christ.

Roy gave the cloth to Roan. She unwrapped the matted hair to show me its male-like appearance. As she pointed to it, something shocking occurred—her voice suddenly changed from female to male. The spirit was manifesting, sensing the threat to its connection with Roan.

I quickly took the dreadlock from her hands and had her sit down. Our adult Bible students gathered around to join me in prayer as I placed the dreadlock at the edge of the wooden floor in preparation for burning it.

Immediately, a large green grasshopper flew in and landed directly on the dreadlock—a strange occurrence that the students later suggested was a manifestation of the spirit itself. As I shooed the insect away, I glanced northward and noticed the sky was completely clear except for a small cloud hovering on the horizon near Angkor Wat Temple, a little more than six miles (ten kilometers) away.

We prayed for protection over ourselves and Roan. After dousing the dreadlock and waist charm with kerosene, I had Roan light a piece of paper, which I used to ignite them. The items began to burn as we continued praying over Roan.

Shortly after finishing our prayers, Roan began speaking in the same male voice I'd heard earlier. She was clearly no longer in control as an entity identifying itself as Ta Essay took over. In Cambodian folklore, Ta Essay is an elderly figure with a long beard and walking stick, playing a similar role to Western depictions of Santa Claus.

I rebuked the spirit in Jesus' name, commanding it to leave immediately and never return. The spirit resisted, continuing to speak through Roan. This spiritual tug-of-war continued for about twenty minutes until Roan's legs began shaking violently. Suddenly, she blinked and looked around in confusion.

"What happened?" she asked, not remembering the past twenty minutes.

This was only my second deliverance experience, and I was still learning the deceptive tactics of evil spirits. I silently prayed for guidance, and the Holy Spirit's gentle voice spoke clearly to my heart: "The spirit did not leave; it is hiding."

I explained this to Roan and prepared to command the spirit out again. When I addressed Ta Essay by name, the spirit immediately retook control, proving the Holy Spirit's discernment correct.

This time, the spirit used Roan's arms and hands as if performing a traditional Khmer dance. Pointing toward the apex of our roof, the spirit declared ominously, "The ruling spirit at Angkor Wat is angry with you."

What happened next stunned everyone present.

A bolt of lightning struck the roof directly above where Roan's finger pointed. Bright flames raced around the edge of the roof as thunder crashed overhead. Simultaneously, rain began pouring down—not gentle tropical rain, but a horizontal torrent driven by fierce winds from the north. The blue sky of just twenty minutes earlier had transformed into a dark, raging storm targeting our exact location. This experience served as clear evidence that Satan and his demon comrades can control the weather and even bring fire down from the heavens.

We quickly carried Roan from the open meeting area into the treatment room, where rain was already seeping through gaps in the wooden walls. There, I continued commanding Ta Essay to leave, asserting my authority in Jesus' name. After another fifteen minutes of spiritual battle, the evil spirit shook Roan's body violently one final time before departing.

When Roan regained awareness, she described seeing "a little man, possibly two feet tall, with long hair. His hands were tied behind his back, and he was walking away from me." It has not been uncommon for people to tell me that when the demon left, they saw a very short person with long hair departing. I find it interesting that certain Hollywood shows feature similarly odd-looking people. It seems that much of what occurs in the spiritual world is mirrored in Hollywood dramas, which are often used by satanic forces to deceive people into believing that evil spirits are either friendly or fictional. They are real and dangerous, and they often do not leave easily.

Some deliverance practitioners will ask demons questions. For example, they might ask what right a demon has to possess its victim, hoping the demon will tell them so they can cancel that right and bar the demon from further entry. Jesus describes Satan in John 8:44 as the father of lies, so it is reasonable to expect that his demonic confederates will also lie. Consulting with a liar is foolishness, and dialoging with a demon is extremely dangerous because they are masters of deception.

I agree that understanding the open door that leads to possession is essential. Sin is often the open door that leads to possession, and identifying the sin and guiding the sinner to repentance can close the door and prevent the spirit from re-entering later. However, clues to the cause of possession should not be obtained from demons. Instead, consult the Holy Spirit directly in prayer. Victims themselves may also be helpful when they are not under the demon's control. In the next part of Roan's story, we learn from Roan herself why other demons were present.

Build Us a House and We Will Leave

The day after Roan's dramatic initial deliverance from the evil spirit calling itself Ta Essay, I sat with her to determine whether additional spirits remained. Something in her demeanor suggested the battle wasn't fully won.

After praying for the Holy Spirit's guidance, I felt prompted to ask about anger in her life. "Do you struggle with anger, Roan?"

She shrugged dismissively. "Sometimes I feel angry, but I don't stay angry for long."

Her husband Roy, who was sitting nearby, laughed loudly. When I questioned his reaction, he explained, "When Roan gets really angry, she stays angry for days." His comment revealed an important truth: Roan's anger had created an opening that evil spirits exploited to gain control of her mind.

As we continued our conversation, Roan recalled another disturbing detail she'd mentioned the previous day—a marble-sized lump on her back that moved up and down when touched. While cysts are common, their movement in response to touch is not. I explained to her that this anomaly pointed to evil spirits as its source.

After praying for protection, I commanded whatever spirit was responsible for the moving lump to leave in Jesus' name. Immediately, Roan lost consciousness and began speaking in a voice different from Ta Essay's but clearly not her own.

"Roy cut all the branches off the Poh tree in our garden," the spirit complained.

The Poh tree—a type of fig—is revered in Cambodia as a dwelling place for spirits. People often tie orange cloth around these trees and make offerings to the entities believed to reside there.

"We had nowhere to live," the spirit continued, "so we entered Roan. If Roy builds us a house, we will leave her."

The spirit was referring to the small spirit houses found outside nearly every Cambodian home—miniature dwellings where traditional spirits allegedly reside. These structures represent a compromise many Cambodians make, acknowledging that evil spirits own the land while humans use it.

As the spirit began dictating dimensions for the house they wanted Roy to build, I cut them off immediately.

"Jesus does not allow you to live in a spirit house," I declared firmly. "In the name of Jesus, leave immediately!"

This time, the spirits obeyed without resistance. Roan regained consciousness and described seeing two small, long-haired beings exiting her body, both with their hands tied behind their backs—a visual confirmation of their defeated state.

With the spirits evicted, Roan's health was restored. She and Roy realized that Jesus possessed greater power than their traditional healers and evil spirits. This revelation led them to choose the Christian faith, and soon we established a small worship group in their village where relatives and neighbors gathered to learn about the God who had freed Roan.

This would be a perfect place to conclude Roan's story—with freedom found and faith embraced. But the actual outcome carries a sobering warning about the persistence of spiritual enemies.

Eighteen months after her deliverance, I visited Roan and discovered a troubling development. She greeted me with unexpected news:

"The evil spirits that had left me returned," she explained. "They asked to be allowed back in."

A chill ran through me. "What did you say to them?"

"I told them I was a Christian now," Roan continued. "They assured me that was not a problem for them. They promised to protect and bless me, so I agreed to let them back in as long as I could continue being a Christian. They re-entered me, and this time my health is great."

I offered to cast out the spirits again, but Roan refused. Eventually, she abandoned her Christian faith entirely. Though her physical health improved under the spirits' influence, her family began experiencing many other problems.

Jesus' words in Matthew 12:43–45 perfectly described what had happened: "When an impure spirit comes out of a person, it goes through arid places seeking rest and does not find it. Then it says, 'I will return to the house I left.' When it arrives, it finds the house unoccupied, swept clean and put in order. Then it goes and takes with it seven other spirits more wicked than itself, and they go in and live there; and the final condition of that person is worse than the first. That is how it will be with this wicked generation" (NIV).

Spiritual Strongholds

During Roan's deliverance, the spirit Ta Essay threatened me, saying, "If you go to Angkor Wat, we will get you." A UNESCO World Heritage site, Angkor Wat was built as a Hindu temple in the early 12th century and later converted to a Buddhist temple by the end of that century. Located just outside Siem Reap City, it is a popular tourist attraction. At the top of the pyramid-like temple are four chambers oriented to the four cardinal directions, each housing a standing Buddha several meters high. Whenever I walked past the southern Buddha, I noticed a rapid diminishment of my strength, akin to what the fictional character Superman would experience when in contact with Kryptonite. This indicated to me a powerful spirit presence; Angkor Wat is a spiritual stronghold of Satan.

About ten years after Roan's deliverance, a visiting friend asked me to accompany him to the temple. I had forgotten the threat made by Ta Essay. As I walked through the outer wall of the temple complex, I felt a heavy weight drop on me, even though nothing was visible. I believe it was the Holy Spirit who reminded me of the threat made a decade earlier. I immediately cried out to God for help, and the heavy weight lifted. Just as when I entered a bookstore selling New Age and Witchcraft books many years earlier, the demons made it clear that, as a Christian, I was not welcome.

I now believe that Christians should avoid such strongholds unless they are on a specific mission directed by Christ. It would be foolish to deliberately walk into a fire ant nest; similarly, it is unwise to intentionally enter a demonic stronghold unless God has sent us to dismantle it.

CHAPTER 3:
Open Doors

The Palm Reader

While working with the Adventist Development and Relief Agency in Siem Reap, Cambodia, a tall Sikh gentleman visited my office. At that time, the United Nations peacekeepers were in town, so I assumed he was connected to them.

"Good morning, sir," he began. "May I have a few moments of your time?"

"Certainly," I responded. "Please sit down."

He sat down across from me and continued with small talk. As he spoke, I felt my energy drain and a wave of nausea and dizziness wash over me. As I sensed my strength fading, reminiscent of a similar experience I had in a bookshop many years before, I realized I was in the presence of a strong demonic power, though I didn't understand why.

It was then that the Sikh man laid his business card on my table and asked to read my palm. I immediately rebuked him in the name of Jesus. He broke out in a sweat, got up, and left. Instantly, my strength returned, and the dizziness and nausea disappeared.

This served as a strong confirmation that those who claim to predict the future are often drawing their information directly from demons. I believe that if I had allowed him to read my palm, I would have opened myself to demonic influence. As Christians, we need to avoid palm reading, tarot card reading, séances, Ouija boards, Eastern meditation, yoga, new age practices, and both white and black magic, among others. Any willingness to engage with demonic powers is an invitation for them to exert control over us.

Instead, seek the Holy Spirit through Bible study and fellowship with other praying, Bible-studying Christians. Jesus promised that "everyone who asks receives, and he who seeks finds, and to him who knocks it will be opened" (Luke 11:10). The gifts of the Holy Spirit are real and powerful to those who know God and are called according to His purpose. It is an unspeakable tragedy when a person chooses the charms of spirit tricksters instead of the gifts of the Holy Spirit. Those who cherish the chalice of demons will hear the King say, "Bind him hand and foot, take him away, and cast him into outer darkness; there will be weeping and gnashing of teeth" (Matthew 22:13).

I Made a Pact with a Legion of Demons

Jon's turbulent teenage years led him to associate with the wrong crowd, plunging him into a life of drug dealing and murder. Fearing what others might do to him, Jon sought protection from traditional Khmer sources: the evil spirits. He made a pact with these spirits through a ceremony, seeking their protection in exchange for his allegiance. While his immediate future felt secure, he was haunted by questions about what would happen after this life.

His Buddhist upbringing taught him that he would be reincarnated, with the quality of his next life determined by his actions in this one. "Do good to receive good, do bad to receive bad." His record as a drug dealer and murderer did not bode well for his future life. Hoping for freedom from his past, Jon began exploring Christianity. In Jesus' teachings, he discovered that through true confession to God, his past wrongs could be transferred to Jesus, the sinless Son of God, who would forgive Jon and bestow upon him His righteousness. Additionally, Jesus promised Jon eternal life without suffering.

Jon also learned that Jesus had sent the Holy Spirit, one of the three in the eternal Godhead, to help man defeat evil in this life while transforming him to become like Jesus in character. In contrast to Buddha's teachings, which brought him despair, Jon found hope in Jesus. Buddha's doctrine of a continuous cycle of reincarnation offered only the hope of escaping suffering by merging with the universe or, more simply, ceasing to exist—an eternity of futility in Jon's view.

At twenty, Jon chose to leave his religious and behavioral past behind and embark on a new life with Jesus. After studying with a Seventh-day Adventist pastor, he publicly professed his new faith and lifestyle, opting for baptism by immersion. Jon had learned from the Bible that baptism involved enough water for one's entire body to be submerged, symbolizing a desire to leave the past behind and embrace a new life in Christ. He confessed his sins of drug dealing and murder and received the forgiveness promised in 1 John 1:9: "If we confess our sins, He is faithful and just to forgive us *our* sins and to cleanse us from all unrighteousness."

This new life brought Jon a joy he had never known, but unbeknownst to him, one lingering issue from his past remained unaddressed.

Jon began attending a Seventh-day Adventist church every Sabbath and grew in his relationship with Jesus. Eventually, his pastor informed him about a four-month training program designed to prepare young people like him to share the hope of Jesus with communities throughout Cambodia. Eager to learn more, Jon enrolled in the training and traveled to the Cambodian province of Siem Reap, where he joined thirty others in deepening their understanding of Jesus and learning how to share their newfound faith with those who had not yet encountered the truth.

From here, I will let Jon continue the story in his own words:

I arrived at a place they called the SALT Centre, named after Jesus' words, 'You are the SALT of the earth.' It was a large property with many trees and ponds, exuding a peaceful atmosphere. As a single man, I was assigned to a large loft above the classroom, which had been nicknamed Heaven, as it was the highest dwelling on the flat property. I soon discovered that I would have a new diet without meat because the teachers believed that the original diet given to man in the Garden of Eden is optimal for today. I initially found it challenging to adjust to my new environment,

The class on evil spirits was intriguing, as I had made a pact with them during my time as a drug dealer.

diet, and people, but despite the difficulties, I was experiencing love like never before.

Our study day began at six in the morning with a thirty-minute presentation on the life of Jesus based on the book *The Desire of Ages*. After breakfast, classes started at 8 AM. The first four weeks of classes deepened our relationship with God and culminated in lessons on how to partner with

Him to heal the sick, raise the dead, and cast out evil spirits. The class on evil spirits was particularly intriguing to me, as I had previously made a pact with them during my time as a drug dealer. What neither I or Teacher Tim realized, was that the evil spirits I once served were about to try and collect on an old debt.

That day, after lunch, I was confronted by a legion of evil spirits seeking revenge. I had pledged my allegiance to them, but then I switched my loyalty to Jesus, their sworn enemy. Now, they demanded payback. They seized my limbs with invisible hands and twisted them, causing me excruciating pain. My fellow students, witnessing my agony, rushed to find our teacher for help.

I remember Teacher Tim arriving at the classroom, gathering the students around me to pray and command the spirits to leave. They placed their hands on me to help restrain my uncontrollable movements while I could only scream in agony. Everyone started praying aloud in our Khmer language, and then Teacher Tim began to command the evil spirits to leave, asserting his authority in the name of Jesus. I heard myself cry out loudly, and then everything went black.

When I regained consciousness, the pain was gone, the spirits were gone, and my friends were praising God for my deliverance. Apparently, I had been unconscious for about a minute.

About an hour later, the same legion of spirits, more furious than before, attacked me with renewed torment. Teacher Tim commanded them to leave again. I cried out loudly and lost consciousness once more. The spirits departed one by one, but there were so many of them!

After several attacks, the spiritual warfare escalated to a new level of intensity. I saw the evil spirits approaching with bows. They were drawing arrows. They began shooting arrows at me, and I screamed, "They are shooting arrows at me!" I collapsed to the floor and started coughing up blood. My friends only saw the pool of blood I had coughed up; they did not see the spirits or the arrows. Once more, Teacher Tim ordered the spirits to leave in the name of Jesus. I cried out again and passed out. When I regained consciousness a few minutes later, I felt fine—no more blood or pain. However, I was confronted by the pool of blood on the tiles, a stark reminder of the battle for my soul. This happened twice that day.

The following day, the attacks continued. During a moment of calm, Teacher Tim asked me what I had done to invite so many evil spirits into my life. I shared with him that I had made a pact with them for protection, but

I thought my baptism had ended my past. Tim explained that I had given these spirits a legal right to claim authority over me and that I had broken my agreement with them. I needed to request the blood of Jesus, shed for me on the cross of Calvary, to cancel the former agreement and transfer legal rights over my life to Jesus, making Him my shield and protector. I then prayed, seeking forgiveness for my pact with the enemies of Jesus, claiming His blood to break the agreement, and asking Jesus to be my shield and protector.

After that prayer, the demons never returned. Jesus became my shield and protector. After completing my four months of study, I was assigned to a region in Cambodia where the people had not heard the good news of salvation in Jesus. I was able to share with them the new life full of joy, love, and hope that Jesus has given me. I shared the truth that I personally experienced: Jesus has all power and authority in heaven and on earth (Matthew 28:18).

The reasons behind demonic harassment or possession are often initially unclear.

The last chapter of this book includes an extensive list of sins that demons may exploit to gain entry and justify harassment.

The knowledge gained from these tools will help close the doors demons have used for entrance. Deliverance is possible when a person prays even alone so long as it is combined with confession and claiming the blood of Jesus to cancel demonic claims of entry. Seng's case, in the next chapter, illustrates this.

CHAPTER 4:
Emotional Gateways

Cloaked with a Grey Shadow

Seng was a fellow student with Jon and the oldest member of our four-month training program. He had taken leave from his job as a policeman to join the program. During our training on preparation for deliverance ministry, I asked Seng and the other students to find a quiet place to pray, asking the Holy Spirit to reveal any unconfessed sins. It was crucial to confess these and be forgiven so evil spirits could not hold any sins against those participating in a deliverance session.

When Jon was attacked by spirits, I called the students to surround him and pray. Seng knelt to my right, placing a restraining hold on Jon's legs. With my eyes closed in prayer, I heard Seng begin to pray as well, but he almost immediately gagged as if he were about to vomit. I opened my eyes to check on him and was surprised to see a grey shadow surrounding Seng. It was obvious to me that he had been attacked by an evil spirit. I instructed some of the male students to take him to another part of the room to pray for him while I focused on helping Jon.

Once Jon was temporarily free from his demonic tormentors, I moved to where Seng was being prayed for. The grey shadow I had noticed earlier was still enveloping him. Apart from that, he appeared normal. I sat in front of Seng and asked what sins he had not confessed that might have given evil spirits access to his life. To my surprise, he admitted he hated his father-in-law.

In 1 John 2:9-11 we are told, "He who says he is in the light, and hates his brother, is in darkness until now. He who loves his brother abides in the light, and there is no cause for stumbling in him. But he who hates his brother is in darkness and walks in darkness, and does not know where he is going, because the darkness has blinded his eyes." This hatred toward his father-in-law had placed Seng outside of God's protection, granting demons a right of entry.

After a brief discussion, Seng prayed, confessing his hatred and asking God for love in place of hate, seeking forgiveness. When he closed his prayer with "Amen," I opened my eyes, expecting the grey shadow around him to be gone; but to my surprise, it remained.

There was still something in Seng's life that demons could use as an excuse to attach themselves to him. I prayed silently, asking the Holy Spirit to reveal what sin Seng was cherishing in his heart. I heard the quiet voice of the Holy Spirit say, "He loves to have power over people." This desire for control is not a Christ-like attribute; rather, it aligns with the traits of Satan and his demonic followers. I looked Seng in the eyes and asked, "Is it true that you love to have power over people?" He hung his head, confessing that it was true. I encouraged him to confess this sin and ask God for a servant's heart. Seng began to pray, confessing his love of power and asking for forgiveness and the servant heart of Jesus. When he closed with "Amen," I opened my eyes and saw that the shadow had vanished. The spirit left, as its assumed legal right had been canceled through confession and subsequent forgiveness from God.

Self-deliverance, as demonstrated with Seng, is achievable when the person being harassed or possessed seeks to free themselves through confession to God and invokes the power of Jesus in their lives. Satan and his evil angels are unwilling to relinquish their prey and often put up a fight, as was the case with Jon. However, when a person confesses their sins, angels of strength come from heaven to assist in their rescue. Seng was conscious and capable of making his own decisions. In his case, it was not necessary to command the evil spirits to leave, as Seng closed the doors of sin, canceling the demons' right of attachment.

The Demon of Self-Pity

The woman they brought to our clinic was unconscious and stiff as a board. Her body was so rigid that when they unloaded her from the trailer, her relatives simply placed her feet on the ground and lowered her to the floor holding only her head. Though her midsection had no support whatsoever, her body didn't bend in the slightest.

Her fists were clenched so tightly that I couldn't unfold her fingers even with considerable force. Yet when I checked her vital signs, everything was paradoxically normal: her breathing was steady, her pulse strong, her blood pressure within healthy range, and her temperature normal. The only abnormality was her complete unconsciousness and the unnatural rigidity of her body.

"How long has she been like this?" I asked her husband and parents.

I learned Srey Ruop had been in this condition for some time. "Nothing wakes her, and her body stays like this—hard like wood."

In Cambodia, when vital signs are stable but consciousness is absent, especially when accompanied by unnatural physical symptoms like extreme rigidity, we immediately suspect demonic influence. Medical professionals in the region know these signs well; sometimes, injection needles will actually bend when doctors attempt to give medications to such patients. Cases like these are typically referred to traditional healers, though some families bring the patients to medical facilities.

I explained to Srey Ruop's family that we would call upon Jesus, the God of heaven, to set her free. After a brief prayer asking for divine intervention, I transitioned to commanding the evil spirits to leave her.

This is precisely when spiritual warfare intensifies—not just in the physical realm, but in the mind of the person attempting deliverance. As I began commanding the spirit to leave, intrusive thoughts bombarded me: "What are you doing? These people have brought this lady for medical help. They're Buddhists—they'll mock your religion when nothing happens. You don't even know if she has an evil spirit. You should take her to a hospital instead."

In such moments, faith in the Holy Spirit's guidance must override both the evidence before us and the doubts Satan plants in our minds. I persisted, commanding in Jesus' name for the spirit causing Srey Ruop's unconsciousness to depart.

Minutes passed with no visible change. I checked her clenched fist again—still rigid, still unresponsive. I continued, repeating the same commands despite the lack of results. Some say we shouldn't be repetitive in prayer, but this wasn't prayer—this was a command for evil spirits to leave, and persistence is often required.

Again, doubts attacked: "There is no demon here," and more insidiously, "Your faith is too weak." I especially despised this second thought because it suggested that this woman would remain under Satan's control because of my inadequacy.

After about twenty minutes of persistent commanding, I noticed a subtle change—her clenched fingers were beginning to soften. Encouraged, I changed tactics and began speaking directly to Srey Ruop herself.

"Can you say the name of Jesus?" I asked her.

Her lips moved, attempting to form words, but she couldn't articulate Jesus' name. And then suddenly, the spirit manifested its presence. Her body relaxed and a male voice spoke through her, identifying itself as her deceased grandfather, who had been blind in one eye. The voice proceeded to identify every person present in the room, stating their names and where they lived— information Srey Ruop couldn't possibly have known.

This created an immediate theological challenge. Srey Ruop's family members, gathered anxiously around her, believed that spirits of the dead continued to exist and interact with the living. This belief contradicts Scripture, which teaches that "the dead know nothing" (Eccles. 9:5 NIV). There were also new Christians present who were still transitioning from animistic beliefs to biblical understanding.

That morning, providentially, I had been reading a book called *The Desire of Ages* which discussed Jesus' death and resurrection. One detail had stood out—how demons had gathered to guard Jesus' tomb, fleeing when He rose on Sunday morning. This gave me a way to test the spirit's identity.

"Were you happy to see Jesus dead in the tomb?" I asked.

The answer came immediately: "Yes!"

"Were you happy to see Jesus rise from the dead?"

This time, there was no answer, just a dark scowl on Srey Ruop's face. I turned to her relatives and explained, "This is not your dead grandfather. Your grandfather was not at the tomb of Jesus 2,000 years ago. This is an evil spirit trying to deceive you."

I don't advocate dialoging with demons, but I believe these questions were inspired by the Holy Spirit and led the demon to reveal its true nature.

The voice began speaking about its poverty, wallowing in self-pity. "I have nothing … no one helps me … life is so hard …" it lamented. I later learned that Srey Ruop and her family were indeed extremely poor.

As I continued commanding the spirit to leave, invoking Jesus' authority, it attempted to negotiate: "If you give her a new sarong and some shoes, I will leave her."

Such bargaining is common in deliverance situations. Like the legion of demons in Gadara who asked Jesus to send them into nearby pigs (see Matt. 8:31, Mark 5:12, Luke 8:32), evil spirits often try to negotiate terms of departure. Jesus sometimes granted such requests, but unless specifically led by the Holy Spirit to do so, I tell spirits that Jesus denies their requests and order them to leave immediately.

This is what I did with the spirit possessing Srey Ruop, and it departed without further resistance. She returned to consciousness, physically exhausted but free from the spiritual bondage.

Two days later, we were urgently called to Srey Ruop's village home. She was fine, but now her one-year-old daughter lay rigid, just as her mother had been. After checking the baby's vital signs and finding them normal, we prayed and commanded the evil spirit to leave her. This time,

I discovered our emotional patterns can create vulnerabilities that spiritual forces exploit.

there was no struggle—the spirit left immediately, and the little girl relaxed, returning to normal.

The attack on this innocent child stirred righteous anger within me. Satan's forces show no shame, even targeting babies to instill fear in adults. Their goal remains unchanged: to inflict as much suffering as possible on God's children, whether they know Him or not.

Through subsequent counseling sessions with Srey Ruop, I discovered how the demonic entity had gained access to her life. As she recounted her experiences and thought patterns, one theme emerged consistently: self-pity. Srey Ruop frequently dwelt on her misfortunes, lamenting her poverty and difficult circumstances. This habitual self-pity had created an opening that the spirit had exploited, entering through this emotional doorway and masquerading as her grandfather.

Her case illustrates a critical spiritual principle: our emotional patterns can create vulnerabilities that spiritual forces exploit. Self-pity particularly creates dangerous openings by focusing on lack rather than God's provision, on suffering rather than redemptive purpose, on comparison rather than contentment.

Jesus has done so much to remove our sin and shame that, regardless of life's difficulties, we must guard against self-pity. Instead, we should "look to the heavens," giving thanks that God bridged the chasm between heaven and earth, allowing us to be called children of the King who will reign with Him eternally. Our earthly trials are momentary compared to the unending joy God has prepared for us (see 2 Cor. 4:17). By cultivating gratitude and contentment, we close doors to the spirit of Self-Pity and strengthen our spiritual protection.

What negative emotional patterns might be creating spiritual vulnerabilities in your life? Could self-pity, fear, or resentment be creating openings for destructive spiritual influences? How about another all-too-common emotion divulged later in this section? Srey Ruop's deliverance reminds us that freedom comes not just from driving evil spirits away, but through transforming the thought patterns that invited them in the first place.

A Demon of Anger

Kuntea wiped sweat from her brow as she knelt in the vegetable garden beside her small house. As a single mother of two and a newly trained Bible worker, she had come to this village on the outskirts of Puok to plant a Seventh-day Adventist church. The work was challenging but rewarding as villagers began to respond to her outreach.

Originally, she had been sent as part of a team with another single mother named Sreyrom. But after a few months, Sreyrom had chosen to return to her home village, leaving Kuntea to continue the work alone. The women had been sent as a team—just as Jesus had sent His disciples in pairs—not just for company, but for mutual spiritual and prayer support. Now isolated, Kuntea became more vulnerable to Satan's attacks.

The first sign of trouble appeared when vegetables began disappearing from her garden—the very food she relied on to feed her children. At first, she was merely puzzled, but as more vegetables vanished, her frustration grew. Eventually, she discovered her next-door neighbor was the thief.

Something dark took root in Kuntea's heart that day. Anger and bitterness began to grow—emotions that when nurtured and replayed in her mind, created an opening through which spiritual darkness could enter.

One afternoon, feeling unwell, Kuntea decided to return to her mother's home to recover. Shortly after arriving, she lapsed into unconsciousness. Concerned, her mother sent a Christian neighbor to ask for my help. When I heard about Kuntea's condition, I gathered my medical equipment and hurried to her mother's house on my motorcycle. Night had fallen by the time I arrived.

Inside the one-room house, an unsettling scene awaited me. Kuntea's mother was preparing offerings for the spirits at the local Buddhist temple, while relatives sat nearby, seemingly unconcerned about Kuntea's unconscious state. After checking her vital signs and finding nothing physically wrong, I faced a dilemma: How could I get an unconscious adult to the hospital? With no vehicle larger than my motorcycle and no cell phone to call for help, I felt stuck.

I began to pray, asking the Holy Spirit for guidance. In that moment of confusion, a clear impression formed in my mind: this was a case of demonic possession. I momentarily questioned this insight—after all, Kuntea was a church planter, a worker for God. But I knew the Holy Spirit's guidance was never wrong, so I began to pray for Kuntea and command the evil spirit to leave her.

Initially, nothing happened. I persisted, repeating, "In the name of Jesus, I command you, evil spirit, to leave Kuntea immediately." Ten minutes passed, then twenty, then thirty, with the same command being issued over and over. Satan often challenges our faith in God's word and the authority we have in Jesus' name, and he was certainly testing me that night.

Doubts assailed me: Was I losing my mind, ordering a spirit out of an unconscious woman when I wasn't even certain one existed? Yet I knew the Holy Spirit had revealed the truth, and despite my doubts, I continued commanding the spirit to leave.

Eventually, Kuntea sat up and began speaking—but in a male voice. I asked Sreysun, the Christian neighbor who had summoned me, to gather other Seventh-day Adventist believers in the village to join us in prayer. Shortly after she left, I felt an immense weight pressing down on my shoulders—a physical manifestation of an evil spirit's attack. Stepping outside, I looked up at the stars and cried out to God to awaken my prayer warriors around the world and prompt them to pray for me. Immediately, the heavy weight lifted.

Back inside the house, I continued commanding the spirit to leave Kuntea. About half an hour later, several other Adventist Christians arrived to join the spiritual battle.

This particular spirit proved talkative, ignoring my commands to be silent and depart. It revealed how Kuntea had become angry with her neighbor for stealing her vegetables and explained how it had exploited this anger to gain entry into her life. The spirit's explanation confirmed what I had observed throughout my missionary career: Satan works diligently to tempt missionaries into sin, then uses that sin to undermine their mission. Kuntea had come to Puok to share Jesus' love, but Satan had set a trap through her neighbor to disrupt God's work.

Around three o'clock in the morning, after the evil spirit complained of feeling increasingly cold, Kuntea vomited—a physical manifestation often accompanying a spirit's departure. Suddenly fully conscious, she looked around in confusion at the group of Christians gathered in her mother's house at this late hour.

"What are you all doing here?" she asked, completely unaware of the previous nine hours.

I explained what had happened and asked about her anger toward the neighbor. Kuntea looked stunned. "How did you know about that?" she whispered.

"The evil spirit spoke about it," I explained. Immediately I encouraged her to pray for forgiveness and challenged her to pray for the neighbor Satan had used to undermine her mission. Kuntea prayed earnestly, and several days later, she returned to her church-planting site to continue sharing Jesus' love.

Some might question: "Is it appropriate to send someone who has been demon-possessed back to plant a church?" Jesus' own actions provide clarity. After freeing the demoniac possessed by a legion of demons, Jesus instructed him to "Go home to your friends, and tell them what great things the Lord has done for you, and how He has had compassion on you" (Mark 5:19). This formerly tormented man became one of Jesus' most effective missionaries.

Demon possession can occur even in Christians when sinful patterns in their lives provide entry points for spiritual darkness. The crucial difference is what happens next: when a believer confesses and genuinely repents, seeking to avoid repeating the sin, God is "faithful and just to forgive us our sins and to cleanse us from all unrighteousness" (1 John 1:9). The door for demons closes, and in God's eyes, it is as if the person had never sinned.

Peter exemplifies this truth. Jesus once rebuked Satan for working through Peter (see Matt. 16:23), and later Peter sinned deeply in denying that he even knew Jesus (see Mark 14:67–71). Yet after repentance, Peter became a powerful missionary for God, recommissioned by Jesus to "feed My sheep" (see John 21:15–17).

Kuntea's story reminds us that Satan specifically targets those engaged in God's work, looking for emotional vulnerabilities like anger, resentment, or isolation to exploit. As Christians, we must guard against opening doors to spiritual darkness while also avoiding condemnation toward those who have suffered such attacks. Ultimately, what matters isn't that Kuntea temporarily fell, but that through Christ's power, she rose again to continue her mission.

What emotional vulnerabilities might Satan be exploiting in your life or ministry? And how might claiming the authority of Jesus help close those doors to spiritual influence?

SECTION THREE:

SATANIC DECEPTION:
Recognizing Demonic Tricks

CHAPTER 5:
Is It Medical or Spiritual?

Demons Can Dance

Chien and her large family lived in a village about forty kilometers (twenty-five miles) from Siem Reap City in the Cambodian countryside. Like others in their community, they were rice farmers, residing in a simple wooden house with palm leaves for walls and a grass roof. Tragically, Chien's teenage daughter had drowned twelve years earlier. Following the tragedy, Chien began experiencing disturbing supernatural manifestations and lost the use of her right leg.

Desperate to be free of the manifestations and regain her ability to walk, Chien called upon several Kru Khmer (traditional healers) at different times, hoping their supernatural powers could alleviate her suffering. They instructed her to set up shelves in her home and prepare items for spirit worship. Chien was to make daily offerings to the spirits in an attempt to appease them, hoping they would leave her in peace. One of the "healers" stood over her, chanting a mantra; while he did so, she coughed up three small snakes that slithered away. However, each intervention by the Kru Khmer seemed only to worsen the supernatural manifestations and impoverish her family.

Eventually, someone informed Chien that there were Christians living on the edge of Siem Reap City who could help her. Traveling by motorbike with her husband, they found the SALT Centre, where my wife and I were conducting training for future Bible workers.

A motorbike carrying a couple in their early fifties pulled up outside our classroom. The woman needed assistance to walk. They introduced themselves as Sem and Chien, explaining that they had heard we could help people troubled by evil spirits. Chien was helped to the steps of the classroom, where she sat down and began describing her problem. I assured her we would help—but first, we needed to teach her about Jesus, the healer.

However, upon hearing the name of Jesus, the spirits took possession of Chien. Instead of being crippled, she stood on both feet, requiring six strong young men to restrain her. Plan A—teaching her about Jesus the healer—was set aside, and Plan B was implemented immediately: we needed to confront the evil spirit directly.

With Chien now restrained, I began commanding the spirit to leave, invoking the authority of Jesus' name. It took about fifteen minutes before the spirit departed, and Chien regained consciousness, albeit still crippled.

I invited her and her husband to stay in our classroom, providing them with meals. Chien was learning about Jesus, but she continued to face periodic attacks. While the demons would leave, there remained an open door for them to re-enter whenever they chose. After several days of listening to messages about Jesus, Chien asked me to accompany her to her home to burn the spirit shelf the Kru Khmer had instructed her to set up. This was no ordinary request; Chien understood that burning the spirit shelf would likely anger the spirits she had been trying to appease. Yet, having experienced the love of Jesus through Wendy, myself, and the students helping her, she concluded that the love of Jesus offered her something far better than what she already had.

The following afternoon, I rode with Sem on a motorbike to his and Chien's home. Our mission: burn the various paraphernalia used in spirit worship and the worship of Buddha. As her husband and I arrived in their home village, Chien was still back in the classroom. I prayed for protection from demonic attack before collecting the spirit shelves and other items, which we took outside to burn. This act symbolized that Chien and Sem were finished with the protection of the spirits and were now pledging their allegiance to the God of heaven.

As the fire consumed the spirit shelves, Chien was asleep in the room where my wife's class was in session. She suddenly sat up, crying, "They are burning me, they are burning me!" Sweat poured down her face. Wendy and the students quickly gathered around the tormented woman, commanding the evil spirit to leave. One spirit departed; doubtless it was the one which had entered as a result of Chien's worship at the spirit shelf which was now destroyed. Another spirit, identifying itself as the eight-armed god, refused to leave. The following day, Chien woke up with burns on her toes despite not being near any fire.

Chien continued to experience periodic attacks from the spirit that identified itself as the eight-armed god. If an attack occurred when I was absent, the students would pray over Chien and command the spirits to leave, but the spirit would not budge. They would then call me, and when I ordered the spirit out, it would leave, albeit temporarily. The students questioned why the spirit would respond when I used the name of Jesus, but not when they did. At the time, I had no answers for them. I felt uncomfortable that this situation made me appear to be someone specially favored by God.

I remembered that Jesus sent out seventy disciples. They were to proclaim the nearness of God's kingdom, heal the sick, and cast out demons. They returned from their mission excited that the demons obeyed them. Jesus cautioned them, "In this rejoice not, that the spirits are subject unto you; but rather rejoice, because your names are written in heaven" (Luke 10:20).

I knew the demons would love to use the students' praise to foster pride in my heart and bring me down. Fortunately, Luke recorded Jesus' words to redirect me from pride in "my" accomplishments and encourage me to instead rejoice in God's love and grace, which accomplishes my eternal life.

About this time, I rose early one morning to pray and prepare a devotional talk on the life of Jesus. As I walked to the classroom, I felt the Holy Spirit tell me that He did not want me to present what I had prepared; rather, I was to speak about Israel's experience with Achan's disobedience to God. I obeyed, sharing how Achan's sin affected the entire army of Israel, leaving them without God's help.

After finishing the talk, the Holy Spirit impressed me to ask the students if there was anything they needed to confess. To my surprise, students began to stand in pairs, confessing differences between them and asking for forgiveness. This continued for about twenty minutes. One student stood alone and confessed that while he had fervently prayed in public, he had done so only to gain praise from others for being spiritual. He sought forgiveness for his pride. Once the confessions were over, I went to breakfast.

While I was away, the spirit attacked Chien again. This time, when the students gathered to pray and commanded the spirit to leave, it departed immediately. When I returned for morning classes, they were all excited about what had happened. That day, they learned an important lesson: if we harbor sin in our hearts, the name of Jesus will not help us cast out evil spirits. However, if we confess our sins to one another and God, putting on the righteousness of Jesus, God can hear and answer our prayers, and the evil spirits will recognize our authority in Jesus.

Paul's advice is fitting: "Let a man examine himself" to see if anything in his life could obscure the presence of God and obstruct the flow of divine power through him (1 Cor 11:28). If such a thing is found, it should be quickly removed by confessing and forsaking sin, lest one's prayers be "hindered" (1 Peter 3:7).

Chien's demon manifested in various ways. On one occasion, when the spirit entered Chien she spun around like a ballerina on her crippled leg. On another occasion, her abdomen rapidly swelled, becoming tight as if she were pregnant with triplets. We gathered around her and ordered the spirit out. Immediately, her abdomen deflated to normal. However, as soon as we stopped praying, it inflated again. The issue was resolved with additional prayer and rebuking the spirit in the name of Jesus.

> *For twelve years, she had blamed herself. This is a satanic lie and opens doors for demon possession or harassment.*

While the spirit would leave temporarily, it became clear that there was an underlying problem that needed to be addressed. We referred to this as an "open door," a reason the spirit could still access Chien and had not left permanently. After she had been with us for about two weeks, I spent time with her to explore how the demon had gained access in the first place.

We discussed events in her life around the time the spirit began manifesting. It was then that she revealed the manifestations had started after her daughter drowned. As I explored with her the impact of this loss, she shared the guilt she carried. For twelve years, she had blamed herself for her daughter's death, believing that if she had been there, her daughter would not have died. I explained that while her presence might have prevented her daughter's death, her absence did not make her guilty.

Many people hold themselves accountable for the death or injury of a loved one, repeating that if they had only done this or that, the tragedy would not have occurred. This is a satanic lie aimed at sinking a person into depression and potentially opening doors for demon possession or harassment. Self-blame cannot reverse the tragedy and may only multiply it as others are negatively affected. When someone feels responsible for such a tragedy, they need to go to God and ask for healing from the scars that Satan tries to inflict through his persistent lies.

Chien and I took this issue to God in prayer, seeking His forgiveness for her self-blame and asking for emotional healing. During that prayer, God performed a miracle for Chien. She was both emotionally and physically healed; her sadness vanished, and her crippled leg was restored. This event closed the door that the spirit had used to enter Chien. She never experienced spirit manifestations again. The leg, which had been a spirit-related problem, returned to normal with the evil spirit's exit. Chien and her family became followers of Jesus, trusting in His power rather than the traditional Khmer healers they had previously relied upon.

Demonic Malaria

Rachana lay unconscious on the mat in our clinic's waiting area, his body burning with fever. His family hovered nearby, their faces shadowed with worry as they explained what had brought them to seek our help at the SALT Center.

"He went to the Kulen mountains to hunt," one of them explained. "When he returned, the fever started. He made offerings to the mountain spirits, thinking he had offended them, but it only got worse. Then he lost consciousness completely."

I nodded, gathering my stethoscope and thermometer. This sounded like a classic case of malaria—a disease I'd treated many times. The mosquito-borne parasitic illness was common among those who ventured into Cambodia's jungles, especially during dawn or dusk when the disease-carrying insects were most active.

As I examined Rachana, skepticism crept into my thoughts. His symptoms perfectly matched malaria: high fever, chills earlier (according to his family), and now unconsciousness as the parasite attacked his system. The family's belief that evil spirits caused his condition seemed like typical animistic thinking—the kind I'd encountered frequently in rural Cambodia, where people attributed malaria not to mosquitoes but to supernatural forces.

Yet something about their mention of the offerings to mountain spirits gave me pause. What if there was more happening here than just a physical disease?

I decided to address both possibilities. First, I prayed for Rachana, asking God to forgive him for making offerings to the mountain spirits—actions that, according to Scripture, opened doors to demonic influence. Then, though part of me felt foolish doing so, I commanded what I called "the evil spirit of malaria" to leave him.

What happened next instantly erased my skepticism. Rachana's eyes snapped open, and he sat up, looking around in confusion. Though still feverish and clearly ill with malaria, his unconsciousness had vanished the moment I addressed the spiritual dimension.

"What happened?" he asked weakly, unaware he had been completely unresponsive just seconds before.

As we administered antimalarial medication, I contemplated what I had just witnessed—a demonstration of how physical illness and spiritual oppression can sometimes intertwine in ways Western medicine doesn't recognize.

The malaria is real, I pondered. *But the unconsciousness was something else—a spiritual component that left when commanded in Jesus' name.*

This case challenged my own Western-trained mind. Native wisdom often contains insights that our compartmentalized thinking misses. Demons can indeed mimic diseases or, as appeared to be the case with Rachana, collaborate with them, amplifying symptoms or adding supernatural dimensions to natural illnesses.

The offerings Rachana had made to appease the mountain spirits had actually granted those entities access to his body and mind. For reasons known only to them, they had chosen to render him unconscious—perhaps to prevent him from seeking proper treatment, or simply to maximize suffering. Thankfully, the authority of Jesus far exceeds that of any demonic power, and at our request, Jesus revokes their authority. In Rachana's case, this allowed the medical treatment to address his physical disease without supernatural interference.

"Will the spirits return?" Rachana wondered as his strength began to return.

"Not if you close the door to them," I said. "Making offerings to spirits—whether you consider them good or evil—grants them permission to act in your life. Jesus offers protection, but He also respects your choices." Rachana nodded thoughtfully.

His case left me with profound questions about the intersection of physical and spiritual realities—questions that would deepen as I encountered more complex manifestations of spiritual warfare in the Cambodian countryside. How many other physical ailments might have spiritual dimensions we're missing? And how might our approach to healing change if we addressed both aspects rather than focusing exclusively on one?

Epilepsy or Demons

"Please help me," Kong said, her young teenage eyes reflecting both hope and fear as she approached me after the Sabbath worship service. "I have epilepsy, and I believe evil spirits are causing it."

I invited her to sit and tell me her story. Kong explained how her seizures had begun shortly after playing near a sacred spirit stone in her village—a small forested area where people left offerings for the deceased village founder, renowned for his magical powers. Children occasionally ventured into this forbidden space, sometimes eating the cakes and fruits left as offerings.

"After I was there, the seizures started," Kong explained. "They're getting more frequent. My sister says your God has power over evil spirits. Could you pray for me?"

The timing of her seizures and her activities around the spirit stone made me consider that her epilepsy might indeed have supernatural origins. I recalled how Jesus Himself had cast a "spirit of epilepsy" from a boy (see Matt. 17:14–18), resulting in his complete healing.

"Kong," I said after sharing the Bible story, "I believe Jesus can help you, too. But I need you to understand something: epilepsy can have both medical and spiritual causes. I'll pray for you, commanding any spirit causing these seizures to leave in Jesus' name. If your seizures continue afterward, you should see a doctor for medical treatment, as it may be a physical condition requiring medication."

She nodded, and I prayed for her, commanding any unseen spirit of epilepsy to leave her in Jesus' name. There was no visible manifestation—no dramatic response that would confirm a demonic presence. I reminded Kong of my earlier advice about seeking medical help if the seizures persisted, and she left with a quiet "thank you."

Months passed without word from Kong. Had she been healed? Had she sought medical treatment? I couldn't be sure. Then one day she reappeared, her expression troubled.

"The seizures are worse now," she said. "They happen more often. I've come to ask you to pray again—to order the spirit out."

I hesitated. "Kong, I suggested you see a doctor if the seizures continued. Why didn't you?"

Her answer surprised me. "Because I knew in my heart it was the evil spirits. But here's what I didn't tell you before—when you prayed for me, I didn't really believe your God had the power to free me. I was just trying everything. But now, after studying Bible passages with my sister, I believe Jesus truly is all-powerful. That's why I came back instead of going to the hospital."

Her words gave me pause. Could her lack of faith have been the reason for the previous failure? Scripture repeatedly shows that faith plays a crucial role in spiritual deliverance and healing. Seeing her newfound conviction, I agreed to pray again.

This time, we approached the throne of grace together. On our knees, we first praised our heavenly Father for His goodness, power, and patience, acknowledging His sovereignty over all spiritual forces. After our prayer of worship, I spoke with authority, commanding the spirit of epilepsy to leave Kong, invoking the blood of Jesus to break its authority, and explicitly forbidding it to return.

Again, there were no visible manifestations—no dramatic signs that something had departed. Just a quiet, peaceful moment between a missionary and a young girl putting her trust in Jesus.

"How will I know if it worked?" Kong asked as she rose from her knees.

"You'll know when the seizures don't return," I replied. "Keep your faith strong, and close all doors to spiritual darkness in your life." Weeks passed, then months. The seizures never returned; the spirit of epilepsy had departed. Kong was now able to face the future with peace instead of fear.

This case raises important questions for those with Western medical mindsets. Was I irresponsible to attempt spiritual deliverance when epilepsy is a recognized neurological condition? Should I have insisted that Kong see a neurologist before attempting prayer?

These questions reflect the compartmentalized thinking common in Western culture, where physical and spiritual realities are rarely integrated. For Kong and others from animistic backgrounds, demons are acknowledged as real entities that can inhabit people and cause suffering. Being told their condition might have a spiritual component isn't traumatizing—it's often a relief that matches their cultural understanding.

I could have sent Kong directly to the hospital for antiseizure medications that may or may not have controlled her symptoms, depending on the demon's whims. But even if the medication had worked, the underlying spiritual issue would have remained unaddressed, potentially manifesting in other ways. Additionally, she would have faced the financial burden of lifelong medication with its possible side effects.

Commanding the evil spirit to leave cost nothing, had no side effects, provided an immediate cure, and resulted in a permanent solution. More importantly, it introduced Kong to the power and love of Jesus Christ—a relationship that would transform far more than just her neurological health.

What if more of our supposedly "purely physical" ailments have spiritual dimensions we're missing? What if our healing approaches are incomplete because we address only one aspect of our integrated human experience? Kong's story challenges us to consider a more holistic understanding of health and healing—one that acknowledges both the physical brain and the spiritual forces that may affect it.

CHAPTER 6:
False Identities

Lucifer is the Son of God!

Not only was Simon's father the head monk at a local Buddhist temple in Siem Reap, Cambodia; some of his extended family practiced magic. This is Simon's story:

"I grew up Buddhist. In 1993, a neighbor returned from a refugee camp in Thailand bringing with her a new religion called Christianity which she had learned about while there. She began sharing how this new faith had brought hope and peace into her life. My older brother was the first to show interest. Later, I joined him in attending the weekly Saturday meetings held in a simple building with a thatched roof. I found the message of a loving God who died on the cross and rose again interesting, but I did not immediately decide to leave Buddhism. My brother, however, became a Christian and later became the local church leader. Eventually I followed him, getting baptized and becoming a member of the Seventh-day Adventist Church.

"The extended family was unhappy with my brother and me, performing spiritual ceremonies to curse us and bring us back to our former beliefs. My brother, more deeply committed to his new faith, was not affected by the magic our relatives conjured, but my relationship with Jesus was not yet strong. My brother was called to attend a training program at the SALT Center, and feeling unwell, I went along, hoping to receive medical treatment. The teacher, Tim, hearing about my illness, gathered the students to pray for me. While I found comfort in their prayers, my condition worsened."

At SALT, Simon was sharing a small wooden house with his brother and a few other students. One night, he woke up shouting and behaving erratically, disturbing everyone's sleep. The next morning the group prayed for him, but there was no change. In the evening, when I spoke with him, he clearly was still not in his right mind.

Simon claimed to be Lucifer and insisted that Lucifer was the true son of God, calling Jesus an imposter and the real Satan. Using the name of Jesus, I rebuked Lucifer and commanded the evil spirit to leave Simon. Immediately, Simon ran toward the fence, crossed it, and headed into the rice fields as darkness fell. The next morning, Simon's brother and some other students searched for him and found him still wandering the rice fields, out of his mind. Eventually, they caught up with him, tied his hands and feet to a pole, and carried him back to the campus, setting him down on the sandy road in front of the classroom. I arrived to find Simon tied to the pole, behaving like a wild animal that had been restrained.

> *I turned to the students, "You heard him; he said 'Yes.' Carry him into the classroom."*

"Do you want Jesus' help?" I asked. Simon immediately responded 'yes' and then 'no.' I repeated the question, and received the same answer. I turned to the students, "You heard him; he said 'Yes.' Carry him into the classroom." Once inside, the students gathered around, pleading with God to set Simon free from the demon controlling him.

One student then stood and looked directly at Simon, saying, "Evil Spirit, I command you in the name of Jesus, come out of Simon." What happened next was undoubtedly a miracle of deliverance. Simon's wild behavior instantly ceased, and he regained control. He was untied and handed a Bible opened to the Psalms and asked to read, ensuring that the demon had truly left. He read serenely from the Psalms as if nothing had happened, with the previous thirty-six hours a blank to him. Today, Simon is the leader of his local church and is strong in the strength of the Lord.

Witchcraft and magic spells are commonly directed at Christians to persuade them to return to their former religions. A Christian firmly rooted in Jesus has nothing to fear from the magic and curses invoked by followers of Satan. Lukewarm Christians, however—those who are more in the world than in Jesus—are very vulnerable when magic is used to summon demons.

My Name is Lucifer

I first met Chantoo and her two children on an island in the Mekong River where they lived in a small bamboo hut. Chantoo suffered from severe arthritis and had been unable to walk for about two years. My purpose for finding Chantoo was to deliver a gift from her mother who lived in Australia where I had just been to visit my sick father. Mission accomplished, I prayed with Chantoo and said goodbye, not expecting to see her again.

About two weeks later, my father passed away and I returned to Australia for the funeral. There I spoke with Chantoo's mother and shared the sad news about her daughter and the poverty her grandchildren faced. The mother asked me to visit Chantoo again on my return to Cambodia.

Chantoo's life was difficult even before she was crippled. She had spent time in a refugee camp in Thailand. There she became a Seventh-day Adventist, but had since backslidden. Now, returning to her home the second time, I noticed Chantoo's right foot was badly swollen and leaking plasma from numerous holes, indicating a tuberculosis infection. I offered to take Chantoo and her children to my home in Siem Reap, about 300 kilometers (185 miles) away, where we could treat the tuberculosis. She was very weak, and I warned her that if she agreed to go to Siem Reap, there was a real possibility she might die along the way. She responded, "I'm going to die anyway, so I will go."

Upon arrival, I told my wife, Wendy, that I had brought home a new patient. She was deeply shocked by how sick Chantoo was and held little hope for her survival. We prayed with Chantoo daily, asking God to restore her health, and we treated her for tuberculosis. Gradually, she improved, her strength returned, and her foot began to heal.

Then one night, one of Chantoo's children came to my home to alert me that Chantoo was behaving strangely. Her face appeared distorted, resembling that of a pig. Although she had nothing in her mouth her actions mimicked chewing tough meat. Her voice took on a male tone, and she no longer identified herself as Chantoo, but as Lucifer. Chantoo was demon-possessed. This demon twisted her face, distorted her voice, and caused her to chew on nothing.

I prayed for Chantoo and commanded the spirit identifying as Lucifer to leave her, but my prayers seemed to have no effect. Over the following days, the spirit would come and go at will. The whole situation tested my faith. I believed God had called us to free people from demons. I confessed all my known sins. Yet when I commanded this spirit to leave, it did not recognize the name and authority of Jesus.

Then for a long time the spirit did not manifest. During this time God showed His care for Chantoo by sending a volunteer sports therapist who helped her learn to walk again. Chantoo attended church every Sabbath, read her Bible, and prayed.

Eventually, the spirit resurfaced. It led Chantoo to visit people in our community, spreading untruths about all the evil things I was doing to her. I had to decide whether to defend myself or ignore the false accusations. I chose to treat Chantoo with respect and ignore her claims, knowing they were untrue. Nothing came of this slander.

One day, Chantoo left and did not return. Her two children were concerned for her. The oldest thought she might have gone to the palace in Phnom Penh, a place she frequented in her childhood. He traveled to Phnom Penh and searched the park in front of the palace but couldn't find her. Deciding to pray, he asked God for help to find his mother. Immediately afterward, he looked up and saw her nearby.

Chantoo returned to Siem Reap with her son, and after a short time, she returned to normal. She worked as a kindergarten teacher for many years until her health began to fail. Throughout those years, the demon never resurfaced. She attended church every Sabbath and gave wonderful testimonies of God's goodness, sharing the miracles He had worked in her life to restore her from her deathbed.

Years later, during the marriage of Chantoo's youngest daughter, her two former husbands attended the ceremony. The emotional trauma of confronting both of them likely reopened the door to spirits. She became possessed again, shouting loudly and being disrespectful to visitors. As before, ordering the evil spirits out proved ineffective.[2]

Chantoo's case exhibits all the hallmarks of demonic possession, yet the demons showed no acknowledgment of Jesus' authority. I confess that after several unsuccessful deliverance sessions, including Chantoo's, I lost my willingness to help free those held captive by Satan. While my faith in God and His purposes remained strong in other areas, my faith in deliverance had waned, and I no longer wanted to be involved.

---

2   Thankfully, the spirits ceased visiting Chantoo after a couple of weeks.

Reflecting on those years, I realize that my desire to withdraw stemmed from wounded pride as a child of God. It appeared that my heavenly Father had failed me. I couldn't understand why God would allow His name and word to be discredited, or at the very least, mocked, by demons refusing to acknowledge His authority. If I were God, I would have burned those demons with fire. I now understand that God doesn't need to protect His name or authority. He is God, and regardless of how many people or demons question or mock His authority, it does not diminish His sovereignty.

It took about two years of God patiently working on my heart before I finally humbled myself. I prayed to God, expressing my willingness to assist Him once again in delivering people from the power of Satan. While I cannot say that every demon-possessed person I have prayed for since then has been delivered, I can affirm that I am at peace with who God is and what He does. I now understand that it is not my role to defend His honor.

God's last-day people are called to be patient with themselves, others, and God. They are to keep His commandments and possess the faith of Jesus (Revelation 14:12). I am learning that the faith of Jesus involves trusting God even when it seems that He fails to intervene; it is knowing always that He is in control and that His thoughts are higher than ours and His ways higher than ours (Isaiah 55:9).

Smoked Baby Talks

Some stories are so disturbing they challenge both your sensibilities and your credulity. What I'm about to share may sound impossible, but I witnessed the aftermath with my own eyes.

Serey was six months pregnant when her belly began to shrink.

In any normal pregnancy, her abdomen should have been expanding as her child grew. Instead, Serey watched her body return to its pre-pregnancy size while something unthinkable developed within her womb. As a traditional healer who practiced black magic, she had opened doors to spiritual realms that most people never encounter. Now, those realms were claiming payment in the most horrific way imaginable.

When Serey reached full term, she delivered a living baby that fit in the palm of her hand.

Cambodian tradition calls these "spirit babies"—the result of demonic possession of an unborn fetus. The cultural practice that followed was even more disturbing than the supernatural pregnancy: Serey smoked the tiny living child over a fire, dried its body, wrapped it in cloth, and kept it as a spiritual consultant.

The shriveled corpse claimed its name was Golden Prince.

"If you care for me for eighteen years," the dried baby would "speak" to Serey during consultations, "I will make you rich."

Champa, a teenager who lingered nearby as I built our fence, was Golden Prince's sister (see her story in Chapter 10). The family's strange arrangement with the supernatural was well known. People would travel to their ramshackle home on the village outskirts, seeking Serey's help with their problems. She would unwrap the tiny mummified form, and Golden Prince would provide answers to their questions.

Eighteen years—that was the demon's timeline for wealth and prosperity. For nearly two decades, Serey and her husband lived in grinding poverty, sustained only by the promise of riches from a spirit that had robbed them of their child's humanity.

When our Bible students shared the gospel with Serey and her husband, the couple showed interest in Jesus. They were willing to destroy their charms and magical paraphernalia. They understood that following Christ meant abandoning their traditional healing practices.

But they refused to surrender Golden Prince.

"He promised to make us rich," Serey insisted. "We cannot give him up."

Here was the essence of demonic deception laid bare: a promise of future wealth in exchange for present horror. The demon had led them to sacrifice their child's normal life, to live in poverty for decades, to endure shame—all for a hollow promise.

The power the mummified Golden Prince held over this family was absolute. The demon that had stolen their son's humanity now held their future hostage with promises of prosperity.

Years passed. The eighteen-year deadline came and went. No riches appeared. Serey and her husband remained on the village outskirts, as poor as ever, until they died in the same rundown house where they had made their deal with darkness.

Golden Prince's promise had been exposed as the lie it always was. But the damage was irreversible. A family had wasted their entire lives chasing demonic fool's gold while rejecting the true riches offered by the Prince of Life.

As I reflected on their tragedy, the parallels to modern deception became clear. Demons make the same promises in Western nations—just in different packaging. Fame, wealth, power, supernatural abilities, special knowledge—all are offered to those willing to compromise their relationship with God.

How many people today are pursuing demonic promises while rejecting divine reality? How many have accepted spiritual counterfeits instead of genuine transformation? How many are trading their souls for treasures that will turn to dust in their hands?

Serey's story forced me to confront an uncomfortable truth: the enemy's greatest weapon isn't obvious evil—it's attractive alternatives to God's plan. Golden Prince didn't appear as a monster. He came as a promise of prosperity, a solution to poverty, a pathway to a better life.

The most dangerous demons aren't the ones that scream and manifest dramatically. They're the ones who whisper promises in the darkness, convincing people to trade eternal treasures for temporal trash.

CHAPTER 7:
Counterfeit Gifts

Speaking in Tongues

The woman's voice was hauntingly beautiful—and utterly terrifying.

Sreymeas spoke in perfect cadences, her words flowing like music, but the language was unknown to anyone. As a teenage housemaid years before, she had eaten a piece of leftover cake. The cake was used in a ceremony and was blessed by a Buddhist monk. Immediately afterward, she began speaking in an unknown language and could speak nothing else for three days. When she regained the ability to speak her native tongue, she could still speak, sing, and write in this unknown language at will.

"My husband is so embarrassed by my unknown language that he is threatening to divorce me. Please help," she pleaded. "Can you tell me what language this is?"

As the only foreigners in the area, Wendy and I often received unusual requests. But this one sent warning signals through my spirit. The circumstances surrounding this "gift" of an unknown tongue—a cake blessed at a Buddhist ceremony, immediate supernatural manifestation, three days of complete linguistic transformation—all were clues. I had been walking with Jesus long enough to recognize the enemy's handiwork.

"Sreymeas," I said, "I believe an evil spirit gave you this language." I explained who Jesus is then told her, "Jesus has the power to take this unknown language away—if you're willing to surrender it."

Though she was a practicing Buddhist, Sreymeas wanted to save her marriage badly enough to give Jesus a chance. She agreed to let me come to her home, burn the spirit items there, pray with her, and order the evil spirits out.

On the appointed day, I arrived with Bee, a praying, God-fearing female believer who could assist with translation. I had another reason for asking Bee to accompany me and that was serve as a witness. Spiritual warfare requires wisdom and accountability. Evil spirits excel at character assassination, and a male missionary working with a possessed woman without a trusted witness is asking for trouble.

> *Evil spirits excel at character assassination, and a male missionary working with a possessed woman is asking for trouble.*

Sreymeas' husband grudgingly allowed us to burn only some of their Buddhist and spirit items, though his scowl made his feelings clear. He gave other items to a neighbor. As we prepared to pray, she revealed more disturbing details: when she cursed people, the curses came true within days. In addition, strangers sought her out for prophecies about their futures.

The pieces fit together like a demonic puzzle. This wasn't just about an unknown language—Satan had been building a supernatural portfolio in this woman's life.

"Jesus wants to set you completely free," I explained. "Not just from the tongues, but from all of it." I prayed with Sreymeas, asking God to set her free from Satan's power. Then I commanded the evil spirit to leave her, claiming the authority of Jesus. I asked Sreymeas if she felt any change. She replied, "No," but mentioned feeling uncomfortable inside. Next, I was more specific, rebuking the evil spirit of speaking in tongues and ordering it to leave immediately.

When I commanded the spirit of false tongues to leave, it fought back. Using Sreymeas's vocal cords, it spoke in that same beautiful, haunting language—but now I heard the deception behind the melody. As the melodious language continued, Sreymeas began to cry. Soon uncontrollable sobs wracked her body.

For two agonizing minutes, I stood in the gap between heaven and hell, claiming Christ's authority over an ancient enemy. Then, suddenly, silence.

Sreymeas was filled with joy. "It's gone!" she exulted. "Before, I had only to think about that language and I would speak it. Now it's completely gone!"

But we weren't finished. Spirits of cursing and fortune-telling still lurked in the shadows of her heart. One by one, we commanded them to leave, and one by one, they fled before the name of Jesus. Sreymeas was very grateful for what we had done for her. Of course, it was not really what *we* had accomplished, but what *God had done* for her. We were merely the channel through which God worked to set Sreymeas free.

Eventually, Sreymeas made the ultimate choice: she surrendered her entire life to the God who had set her free and followed Jesus into the waters of baptism.

Her story illustrates a crucial lesson: demons are master counterfeiters. They study God's genuine gifts and create convincing imitations designed to deceive even believers. The gift of tongues and the gift of prophecy had been counterfeited in Sreymeas' life. Traditional healers with their direct connection to the spirit world often manifest the counterfeit gifts of healing and casting out evil spirits. These spiritual gifts and others can be, and often are, mimicked by fallen angels who have six thousand years of practicing deception. This is why Jesus warns us:

> Beware of false prophets, who come to you in sheep's clothing, but inwardly they are ravenous wolves. *You will know them by their fruits.* Do men gather grapes from thorns, or figs from thistles? Likewise, every good tree bears good fruit, but a corrupt tree bears evil fruit. A good tree cannot bear evil fruit, nor can a corrupt tree bear good fruit. Every tree that does not bear good fruit is cut down and thrown into the fire. Therefore, by their fruits you will know them.
>
> Not everyone who says to me, "Lord, Lord," will enter the kingdom of heaven, but only he who does the will of my Father who is in heaven. Many will say to me on that day, "Lord, Lord, did we not prophesy in your name? And in your name cast out demons? And in your name perform many wonders?" Then I will declare to them, "I never knew you; depart from me, you who practice lawlessness." (Matthew 7:15-23, emphasis added)

Spiritual gifts from the Holy Spirit can be powerful tools for building up God's kingdom. However, counterfeit spiritual gifts from demonic sources, while appearing good, can be used in Christian churches to tear apart God's kingdom.

I've counseled with many who had first sought help for their demonic problems from pastors who prayed over them in unknown tongues. These sufferers told me how their situations worsened after such interventions. My advice to those seeking freedom from demons is this: find God-fearing individuals who carefully adhere to every part of the Word of God.

As I turned homeward that day, one question burned in my mind: If demons could imitate God's gifts, how many believers might be deceived into thinking their supernatural experiences came from heaven when they actually originated in hell?

A later experience showed that false spiritual gifts are given, not just to Buddhist villagers in Cambodia, but to people in Western cultures who consider themselves devoted Christians.

Her Writing Hand

Across the world, her husband reached out to me through the Internet with growing concern. Ever since his wife had asked a Pentecostal preacher to help her speak in tongues, she had been experiencing disturbing manifestations—disturbing to her husband, that is. Whenever she sat down with notebook and pen, strange mouth movements would begin, accompanied by vocal sounds, while her hand wrote messages she claimed came from heaven.

Her husband sent me photos of the handwritten notes. As I studied them, every spiritual alarm in my soul began ringing. The messages contained just enough biblical truth to seem authentic, but they were laced with subtle errors that twisted divine revelation into demonic deception.

Here was a new category of spiritual warfare I was only beginning to understand: demonic attachment.

Unlike full possession, where evil spirits take complete control, attached demons operate from the shadows of a person's life. They don't manifest overtly or announce their presence with supernatural displays. Instead, they whisper thoughts that feel like personal insights, encourage behaviors that seem merely like personality traits, and influence decisions in more natural ways.

The Baptist woman wasn't possessed—she was deceived. A demon had attached itself to her spiritual hunger and was feeding her contaminated supernatural experiences disguised as divine gifts. She believed she was growing closer to God while actually moving deeper into demonic bondage. I continue to pray for this woman and all like her who suppose they are under the influence of the Holy Spirit without realizing what's influencing them is an evil spirit. "And no marvel; for Satan himself is transformed into an angel of light" (2 Cor. 11:14).

The Baptist woman's experiences opened my eyes to a terrifying possibility: How many believers were living with demonic attachments they couldn't even recognize?

> *Sometimes, even Christians could be deceived into demonic attachments.*

As I reflected on years of deliverance ministry, patterns began to emerge. Negative personality traits that seemed like character flaws often had spiritual components. Self-destructive behaviors that appeared to be personal choices frequently involved supernatural influence. Addictions that felt like medical conditions sometimes included demonic elements that medication alone couldn't address. Sometimes, even Christians could be deceived into demonic attachments.

The demons I had encountered in dramatic deliverance sessions—spirits of pride, self-pity, cursing, false tongues, abandonment—these same entities could operate through subtle attachment rather than obvious possession. They might not have legal rights to control a person completely, but they could still plant thoughts, encourage destructive patterns, and gradually shape character in ways that opened doors for deeper influence.

The Girl with Sapphire Eyes

The teenage girl had gathered quite an audience. A circle of young men listened with rapt attention as she spoke with unusual passion and authority. Curious about what was drawing such focused interest, I walked closer to listen to what she was saying.

"Christians need to wake up because Jesus is coming soon!" she urged, her voice intense with conviction. Her message was biblically sound, even powerful—exactly the kind of truth I would want shared. But something about her troubled me deeply: her pupils glowed an unnatural, brilliant sapphire blue.

The setting was a vacant lot in Phnom Penh, outside a large tent pitched for a series of Christian evangelistic meetings scheduled to begin that evening. The young woman, like many others, had arrived on one of the trucks that transported attendees from surrounding areas.

As the event's prayer team leader, I had stepped outside our tarpaulin-walled prayer room to observe the gathering crowd when I noticed this charismatic young woman and her captivated audience. Something about the scene felt spiritually discordant—truth being spoken, but with an unsettling evil presence behind it.

When the meeting began, her impromptu sermon ended and I returned to the prayer room to join my team in interceding for those who would speak and hear God's Word that night. The next evening, I noticed the same young lady again. Approaching to introduce myself, I learned her name was Lina. Her sister accompanied her, and both had been studying the Bible with a local worker. As we spoke, those eerily luminous sapphire eyes held my gaze.

After the third night's meeting, I spotted Lina attempting to speak with the evangelist, Dr. Mike Ryan. The language barrier was creating obvious difficulty, so I approached to help translate. Her request surprised me: she wanted permission to go on stage and address the audience about Christians needing to "wake up" before Jesus returned.

As I gently led her away from Dr. Ryan, explaining why this wouldn't be possible, I felt a sudden, oppressive weight descend on my shoulders—the unmistakable sensation of an evil attack that I had experienced in previous encounters with demonic forces. My voice grew hoarse as I turned to Lina and commanded the evil spirit to leave her.

At that precise moment, my friend Pastor Scott Griswold happened to pass by. I explained in my strained voice that the young woman had a demonic presence and needed prayer. We escorted her to the prayer room, where our team immediately began interceding. Shortly afterward, Lina's sister arrived to announce their truck was departing, and Lina left with her. By then, my voice had returned to normal.

For the next twenty-two hours, I questioned my actions. Had I overstepped? This young woman was preparing for baptism and seemed to have the right message and motives. Yet I had ordered an evil spirit out of her without her request. What if I had misread the situation entirely?

The following evening, before the meeting, Lina entered the prayer tent and approached me directly. "How did you know I had an evil spirit in me?" she asked. I noticed immediately that her pupils were now a normal black color, no longer that unsettling sapphire blue. Relief washed over me as I silently thanked God for the discernment and courage He had provided the previous night.

Months later, I was delighted to see Lina and her sister attending a small church on the outskirts of Phnom Penh, both growing in their relationship with Jesus.

This encounter illustrates one of Satan's most cunning strategies: using partial truth as a vehicle for spiritual deception. Lina's message about Jesus' return wasn't wrong—it was biblical and timely. The problem wasn't the content but the evil source behind it. Scripture warns us that "Satan himself transforms himself into an angel of light" (2 Cor. 11:14) and that in the last days, there will come "false prophets" who perform signs and wonders to "deceive, if possible, even the elect" (Matt. 24:24).

In Lina's case, a demonic entity was using biblical truth as a Trojan horse, attempting to establish credibility through correct doctrine while planning to introduce subtle deceptions later. Those glowing sapphire eyes were the physical manifestation of a spiritual reality that most observers missed as they were focused on her compelling message.

Normally, I would not confront a demon without being asked by the affected individual or their family, but the spiritual oppression I felt and the clear physical sign of demonic presence prompted immediate action. The restoration of Lina's natural eye color confirmed what the Holy Spirit had revealed.

Lina's story raises important questions for all believers: How can we discern when truth is being used as a vehicle for deception? What signs might indicate that a spiritual message, though seemingly correct, comes from a deceptive source? And how can we maintain spiritual sensitivity without becoming paranoid or judgmental?

The answers lie in maintaining a close, daily relationship with Jesus Christ, studying Scripture diligently, and developing spiritual discernment through prayer and obedience. Jesus promised that His sheep would know His voice (see John 10:27)—an ability that grows stronger as we walk with Him daily.

For those engaged in ministry, Lina's case underscores the critical importance of spiritual discernment beyond theological correctness. We must be attuned not just to what is said, but to the spirit behind the words. The salvation and spiritual health of others may depend on our willingness to act on God's promptings, even when doing so feels uncomfortable or risks misunderstanding.

The Blood-Curdling Scream

The video on Sharon's phone made my blood run cold.

Her father stalked through their home like a predator, cursing her with words so vile they seemed to poison the air itself. His eyes held a rage that belonged to something far older and more malevolent than human anger. As a primary school teacher, Sharon should have been safe in her own home. Instead, she was documenting evidence of her own father's possession.

"Will you come?" she asked after showing me the footage at the Army of Youth Congress in Malaysia. "After this event ends?"

I had agreed to help before I fully understood what we were walking into.

Sharon's house felt heavy with oppression the moment we arrived. Her father took one look at our group—Sharon, her mother, their pastor, Wendy, and me—and roared off on his motorbike. Apparently, demons could sense a prayer meeting forming.

The spiritual battlefield was evident all around us. In the dining room, empty beer cans were arranged in a pyramid like some twisted shrine. On the tile floor, curses against Sharon were handwritten in bold Chinese characters.

We knelt in the living room, five believers agreeing in prayer for a man who had fled rather than face the light. For several minutes, our intercession felt powerful and unified. We were asking God to break chains, to set a captive free, to restore a father to his daughter.

Then Sharon screamed.

The sound that tore from her throat wasn't human. It was the howl of something trapped and furious, the voice of hell itself using her vocal cords. I opened my eyes to see her face twisted in anguish, beautiful features contorted into something nightmarish.

The demon had struck the innocent while we prayed for the guilty.

"In the name of Jesus, leave her!" I commanded immediately, but the spirit held fast. Sharon's screams continued, each one like a knife through my heart. Here was a godly young woman who taught children, who had sought help for her father's condition, and now she was paying the price for her family's spiritual compromise.

Her pastor mumbled something about another appointment and fled. Perhaps he had never seen the true face of evil. Perhaps he couldn't handle the reality that spiritual warfare sometimes erupts in the middle of prayer meetings. Whatever his reason, he left us to face the battle without him.

But Jesus had not fled. For long, agonizing minutes, her mother, Wendy and I stood guard over Sharon's soul, commanding the invader to leave, claiming Christ's blood over her mind and body. Then the screams stopped, the twisted features softened, and Sharon could speak again. The demon was gone.

The transformation was instantaneous and complete. In fact, Sharon and her mother took my wife and I out to dinner. It was as if the possession had never happened. Sharon seemed back to her normal self.

But the war wasn't over.

Several years later, Sharon approached me again at another spiritual warfare conference. This time, the request was for herself. Every time she tried to pray, her face would twist, making speech nearly impossible. The enemy had returned with a different strategy—not dramatic possession, but subtle harassment designed to cut off her lifeline to heaven.

Our prayer team gathered around her, and she shared a troubling history: childhood levitation, supernatural occurrences in her home, a fascination with spiritual powers that she had used for her pleasure. Like many believers, Sharon wanted salvation through Jesus but had never fully severed her ties to the supernatural realm that had entertained her as a child.

"I want to be free," she whispered as her face began to contort again. "But I also ... enjoyed some of the experiences."

There it was—the heart of the problem. Sharon stood at the crossroads that challenge every believer: Would she choose the clean, narrow path of following Jesus alone, or would she try to walk both sides of the spiritual fence?

This time, when we commanded the face-twisting spirit to leave, there was no blood-curdling scream. The demon departed after fifteen minutes, leaving Sharon able to pray normally for the first time in months.

I thought her story was finished. I was wrong.

Two weeks later, the spirit had returned. Sharon's compromise had been exposed: while she wanted freedom from demonic harassment, she struggled to completely surrender the supernatural experiences that gave power to demons in her life. As I reflected on Sharon's struggle, uncomfortable questions pressed against my own heart: How many believers today are trying to serve two masters? How many want Jesus as Savior but refuse to let Him be Lord of everything in their lives? How many churches are harboring people who love God at church but dabble on enchanted ground the rest of the week?

When Jesus said we cannot serve two masters, He was addressing a very real problem people face today. Many individuals desire salvation through Jesus but often unwittingly engage with evil spirits, enjoying the supernatural powers demons provide. Evil spirits have six thousand years of experience in deception. They use music, movies, video games, yoga, meditation, anime, creepypasta, porn, sexual sin, and more to lure Christians into using their power or making secret pacts with them. These pacts remain secret because the Christian is unaware of their existence. Deceived Christians believe that their relationship with God is intact, even while they have attachments to unseen demons.

If you are a Christian and the Holy Spirit is prompting you about something, perhaps an activity mentioned above, you may have demonic attachments. Jesus died on the cross of Calvary to break those attachments. Go to God, confess your sins,[3] ask for victory over sin, and claim the blood of Jesus to break any agreements you have made (knowingly or unknowingly) with demons.

Remember, demons are cunning and will do their utmost to convince you that nothing has changed in your life. They will try to persuade you that the addictions you have confessed remain so that they can keep you enslaved. When we confess our sins with a genuinely repentant heart, we are born again. If we are born again, the addiction is gone. The victory belongs to Christ; everything has changed.

---

3   See 1 John 1:9.

SECTION FOUR:

DEEPENING THE MINISTRY:
Advanced Lessons

SECTION FOUR

DARKENING THE MIND'S EYE

Advanced Lessons

CHAPTER 8:
Healing Inner Wounds

Burn The Oxcart

"You must destroy it." The traditional healer's voice was firm as he pointed at the wooden oxcart beneath the desperate family's house. "Cut it up and burn it completely. It's your son's last hope."

Kuon's father stared at the family's prized possession. The oxcart provided not only essential transportation but also future income potential. It was the final demand in a series of increasingly costly "spirit prescriptions" that had stripped the family of both money and dignity.

First, it had been a multi-tiered spirit shelf that must be installed in their home and the cost of daily appeasement offerings to be placed there. Then the demolition orders began. The central hardwood support pole was inhabited by an evil spirit and must be removed; now the bamboo replacement left the two-story structure at risk. Next, the spirits demanded removal of their property's fence. Most recently, the pad around their well—the only concrete well pad in the village—had been smashed to pieces with a sledgehammer to appease the spirits.

Despite every sacrifice, their eighteen-year-old son continued to deteriorate. Now he lay helplessly on one side, his hair matted into a dreadlock, hovering at the threshold of death.

"No," Kuon's father finally decided, his voice quiet but resolute. "I will not destroy the oxcart." Instead, he made a decision that would change everything—he would seek help from the Christians at the nearby SALT Center.

He appeared at our classroom door that afternoon, desperation etched on his face. "My son is dying," he explained, describing Kuon's condition and all they'd been through in the battle to save him. "Can you help us?"

> *What caught my attention next was strange even by Cambodian standards.*

I gathered our students, and we walked the short distance across the rice fields to their home. The precious oxcart sat beneath the house, a silent witness to the family's stand against superstition. The steps leading to the first floor were round poles without handrails, making our ascent precarious.

The moment I entered the house, I sensed it—a heaviness in the air despite the open eaves that ordinarily allow free airflow. It was a sure sign that evil spirits were in residence. The spirit shelf loomed opposite the doorway, covered with offerings. To the left lay Kuon, emaciated and weak.

What caught my attention next was strange even by Cambodian standards—a pigeon perched atop the wall above Kuon's head, with droppings accumulated on the floor next to him. When I inquired about the bird, the family explained it had appeared shortly after Kuon fell ill and had remained in the spot above his head ever since. Hearing this, I realized it was linked to the spirits troubling Kuon.

I consulted with the Holy Spirit and devised an action plan, then turned to Kuon's father. "With your permission," I explained, "we will burn the spirit shelves, the spirit flag, Kuon's waist charm and wrist strings, plus his dreadlock and—if we can catch it—the pigeon." A comprehensive spiritual housecleaning was needed to remove the access points used by the spirits who tormented his son. "Then we will ask Jesus to drive the evil spirits away."

After all he had experienced, Kuon's father was growing skeptical of the traditional beliefs he had been raised with. He knew little about Christianity, but our services—in contrast to those of the traditional healer—were free. He took the risk and gave his approval.

The students gathered around as I prayed for wisdom and protection, then they scrambled into action. Several worked to dismantle the spirit shelf and carry it outside to be burned. Another climbed up to retrieve the red flag, hung at the roof's apex during construction to invite a "caretaker" spirit. The pigeon, unfortunately, escaped our attempts to capture it.

Inside, the air remained thick. Walking around the house, I loudly claimed the name of Jesus as my authority and ordered the spirits to leave and never return. The transformation was immediate and palpable. The oppressive heaviness dissipated, replaced by normal airflow.

Next we gathered around Kuon and began to pray. The students felt their body hair stand on end; an invisible weight pressed down on my shoulders. These were physical manifestations of the spiritual battle taking place as the remaining spirits tried to make our visit as unpleasant as possible.

We cut the dreadlock from Kuon's hair and removed the waist charm and red wrist strings, adding them to the fire outside. Then, with the authority Jesus grants His followers, we commanded the evil spirits to leave Kuon's body.

Kuon's father looked on with hope in his eyes as we tied a hammock to a pole and prepared to transport his son to our health clinic.

There our examination confirmed my suspicion—advanced tuberculosis of the lungs, a serious but treatable condition requiring an eight-month course of medication. Based on experience with similar cases, I knew it would take about two months before Kuon would regain enough strength to walk home.

"This treatment time serves another purpose," I explained to the students. "It gives us the opportunity to introduce Kuon to Jesus—the one who has set him free from evil spirits and is working alongside the medication to restore his physical health."

What unfolded over those next two months exceeded everyone's expectations. Kuon's tuberculosis symptoms disappeared. He gained weight and strength, eventually taking his first tentative steps. But more significant than his physical recovery was his spiritual awakening—a growing hunger to know the Jesus who had saved him when all else had failed.

The transformation didn't end with Kuon. His sister also embraced faith in Jesus, and both were later baptized. When Kuon eventually married, he led his wife to Christ as well. They raised four children who received an education in our Christian school.

Though the evil spirits never returned, tuberculosis did. Each recurrence left more scarring on Kuon's lungs. During his third bout with the disease, Kuon recognized that his lungs could no longer sustain him. Facing death with remarkable peace, he called us to his home with one final request.

"Please dedicate my family to Jesus," he said, his breathing labored, but his eyes clear. "My only desire is to see my wife and children again when Jesus returns."

Shortly afterward, Kuon died peacefully, his hope firmly anchored in Christ's promise of resurrection.

I've often reflected on what might have happened if Kuon's father had followed the traditional healer's final demand to destroy the oxcart. Instead, his refusal became the turning point that led his son—and eventually other family members—from darkness to light. When Jesus instructed His disciples to "Heal the sick, cleanse the lepers, raise the dead, and cast out demons," adding "freely you have received, freely give" (Matt. 10:7–8), He established a pattern of ministry that continues to transform lives today.

The price for Kuon's freedom wasn't the destruction of an oxcart—it was paid by Jesus on the cross of Calvary, where He claimed the right to set people free from both physical disease and demonic oppression. What is there in your life that Jesus might want to free you from today?

Coming Out of Deep Depression

Ratana began studying the Bible with a Seventh-day Adventist pastor in her home province in Cambodia. Before fully committing her life to God, she married a soldier and moved to Siem Reap Province. Her drunken soldier husband treated Ratana with disrespect, beating her daily.

Ratana was descending into deep depression from the constant emotional and physical abuse. One day, after a particularly severe beating, she found herself many kilometers from home, with no recollection of leaving the village. Realizing she needed mental help, she decided to go to Siem Reap City for assistance at the hospital. This prepared the way for God to intervene on Ratana's behalf.

The motorcycle driver who took her to the hospital dropped her off outside the rehabilitation ward. Upon entering, she spoke to a staff member about her problem and asked for help. Recognizing her deep depression, he agreed to assist her. Instead of taking her to the psychiatric ward of the hospital, he offered to take her to our house. While we had never met him before, this Christian man had heard how people who sought help from us for demon possession were delivered. Ratana, having learned about Jesus before her disastrous marriage, agreed to go.

We welcomed Ratana into our home, and over the next several days, we spent time in prayer, seeking God's deliverance from her deep depression. Understanding that physical, emotional, and sexual violence can create openings for demons to enter the lives of the abused, we worked with Ratana to close those doors one by one. As we prayed together, we asked the Holy Spirit to reveal any sins she had committed or that had been committed against her. One by one, the Holy Spirit brought to light aspects of her life that needed to be addressed. Ratana confessed her sins and sought healing from God for the scars left by those sins and the abuse she had endured. We claimed the blood of Jesus to close the doors opened by abuse, idolatry, and other sins as the Holy Spirit brought various issues to her mind.

Ratana's transformation was a miracle of God's grace. She had arrived at our home deeply depressed, struggling to speak and think clearly. Gradually, over three days, her depression lifted. Although no demons manifested during this time, they were losing their grip on her. By the end of the third day, Ratana was transformed, happy, and full of energy. She chose to return to her parents' home instead of going back to her intoxicated husband.

As deliverance practitioners, we should assist those who are afflicted in shifting their focus away from self and defeat, directing them toward the love and power of God and His willingness to facilitate their victory. Involving the afflicted in their deliverance is possible when they are not directly under the control of demons. Ratana was not possessed but was experiencing significant demonic harassment due to her depression. By guiding Ratana through the process of finding freedom in Jesus, she was able to realize the liberation that had previously eluded her. James instructs, "Submit yourselves therefore to God. Resist the devil, and he will flee from you. Draw nigh to God, and He will draw nigh to you. Cleanse your hands, ye sinners; and purify your hearts, ye double-minded.... Humble yourselves in the sight of the Lord, and He shall lift you up" (James 4:7–10).

Caterpillars in the Brain

Nieng's twisted foot was the least of her problems.

Polio had left her with physical deformities that kept her single in a culture where marriage was everything. The Pol Pot regime had stolen her childhood education, leaving her illiterate and isolated. But the spiritual torment that began in her twenties made her physical and social challenges seem insignificant by comparison.

It started with an "angel."

Night after night, a being of light appeared in her bedroom, requesting sexual intimacy. When Nieng refused these advances, the entity's true nature revealed itself through excruciating pain that felt like caterpillars chewing through her brain tissue.

Imagine trying to sleep while invisible creatures devoured your brain from the inside. Picture waking each morning wondering if this would be the day the pain finally drove you insane. Consider the isolation of explaining to anyone that an angel was sexually harassing you while demons consumed your thoughts.

Nieng was trapped in a nightmare that most people would dismiss as mental illness.

When newly trained Bible workers moved to her village, they heard whispers about a woman whose supernatural problems defied medical explanation. Their prayers for her brought no immediate relief, but they offered something more valuable than instant healing: hope that their teacher might know how to help.

Nieng arrived at our training center carrying years of pain in her twisted body and caterpillar-infested brain. We prayed over her repeatedly, commanding the spirits to leave, but they seemed entrenched like squatters who refused eviction notices. However, we offered her something demons couldn't attack: education.

For the first time in her life, Nieng learned to read.

While spiritual battles raged around her, she quietly conquered literacy. Letter by letter, word by word, she built bridges to a world that had been closed to her since childhood. When she could finally read the Bible for herself, something shifted in the spiritual realm.

The transformation was gradual, like sunrise after a long night. The brain-chewing sensations diminished. The nocturnal visits became less frequent. Slowly, steadily, the torment that had defined her existence began to lose its grip.

Today, twenty-five years later, Nieng remains an avid Bible student. The woman who once writhed in spirit-induced agony now serves as living proof that no torment is too great for God's healing power.

Her deliverance taught me crucial lessons about the patient process of spiritual warfare. Sometimes God works instantly, with dramatic manifestations and immediate freedom. But sometimes He chooses the slower path of gradual transformation, using ordinary means like education and community to accomplish supernatural ends.

The demons that tormented Nieng probably expected her to give up, to accept her fate as a spiritually harassed outcast. They didn't anticipate a woman who would learn to read in order to study the very book that contained the keys to her freedom.

When Wendy asked Nieng to stay on as our cook, she gained more than employment—she found her calling. Having experienced God's power to deliver from satanic harassment, she became a valuable member of my deliverance team. There's something powerful about having former victims on your spiritual warfare team. They possess unshakeable faith in God's ability to set captives free because they've lived that miracle themselves.

Nieng's presence in deliverance sessions carried a unique authority. When demons tried to convince new victims that freedom was impossible, they had to contend with a living testimony kneeling in the room. Her very existence proclaimed that the worst spiritual torment could be overcome through patient faith and divine grace.

But her story also challenged my understanding of God's timing. Why didn't He deliver her instantly when we first prayed? Why allow the gradual process instead of immediate freedom? What purpose did her extended suffering serve?

The answers came as I watched Nieng minister to others. Her prolonged battle had forged a depth of compassion and understanding that instant deliverance couldn't have created. She knew intimately what it felt like to pray without apparent answers, to hope when circumstances suggested hopelessness, to trust God when relief seemed impossible.

Every person who found freedom through our ministry benefited from Nieng's hard-won wisdom. Her story proclaimed that if God could deliver a polio-crippled, illiterate woman from decades of demonic torment, He could deliver anyone.

Srey Day's Abandonment & Anger

Some deliverance practitioners believe demons attach to specific body parts based on their specialties. While I have limited evidence for such precise mapping, Srey Day's case supports this possibility.

Abandoned by her mother in early childhood, Srey Day had grown up with learning difficulties and periodic violent outbursts. Occasionally, she experienced what seemed like panic attacks—difficulty breathing combined with sharp pain in her upper right chest. After one Wednesday night prayer meeting, I witnessed another episode and sensed demonic activity.

Abandonment was the root issue that eventually led to demons attaching to her life.

"In the name of Jesus, leave her!" I commanded, and Srey Day immediately lost consciousness. For ten minutes, I continued commanding the spirit to depart until it finally left, and she regained consciousness without pain or breathing difficulties.

As we walked to her home, both of us concluded that abandonment was the root issue that eventually led to demons attaching to her life. When I checked a list of demonic attachments I had recently received, I discovered that the upper right chest was listed as the attachment point for abandonment spirits.

Whether that specific mapping was accurate mattered less than the core principle: demons can sometimes use unhealed emotional wounds to create opportunities for attachment. Abandonment leads to anger. These emotions are normal, yet they must be dealt with under the guidance of the Holy Spirit. When anger leads to resentment or hatred and the heart is hardened against the Holy Spirit's influence, it provides an opening for evil spirits to become influential in a person's life. Srey Day's abandonment made an opening that evil spirits exploited for years, causing physical symptoms and emotional distress.

The solution was emotional healing from the Holy Spirit. The following day, I met with Srey Day at her home to discuss her abandonment issues in greater detail. She expressed anger toward her mother for putting her in foster care. At the time she was given up, she was old enough to remember her mother but not old enough to understand the reasons for her placement. In addressing demonic issues, it is more important to understand the emotional reaction to the situation than to know all the details. Healing the emotional scars left by abandonment is key to closing the doors that allow demons to take advantage of such traumatic events. Srey Day needed to forgive her mother despite not understanding the circumstances of her abandonment. She needed to experience her identity as a beloved daughter of the God of Heaven. She needed the Spirit of Jesus to heal the trauma that had granted demons their foothold.

Together we prayed for divine healing for her pain and anger. As God addressed the root cause of abandonment, the doors that had allowed demonic attachment were closed, and the spiritual oppression ended.

This experience taught me that effective spiritual warfare must address both the demonic symptoms and their underlying causes. Commanding spirits to leave without healing the emotional wounds leaves a hole in the soul through which a demon may tempt and eventually re-enter. Healing psychological wounds through faith in the power of the Holy Spirit blocks evil spirits from slipping back into a person's life.

CHAPTER 9:
Special Cases

My Boy Wakes Up Screaming Every Night

"My boy wakes up screaming every night at ten o'clock," Seng's father confided, worry and exhaustion etching lines around his eyes. "It's like clockwork—something terrifies him at exactly that same time. We've had pastors pray, but nothing changes."

We stood in the shade at a church camp meeting, watching two-year-old Seng play happily with other children—a normal, energetic toddler during daylight hours. Looking at him, you'd never guess the terror that gripped him nightly.

"Why do you think my prayers would be different from the pastors who have already prayed?" I asked gently.

His answer reflected both desperation and faith: "I know you keep a close relationship with God, and you have experience dealing with evil spirits."

That evening, I went to the family's cabin where Seng was already sleeping peacefully on his mat. I knelt beside his parents, near their sleeping child, his innocent face relaxed in slumber. What unseen force disturbed this little one at the same hour each night? And why would spiritual darkness target a child raised in a loving Seventh-day Adventist home?

In my prayer, I first praised God for His goodness in blessing this family with a son. I asked that the Holy Spirit fill Seng even at his young age, and that he would one day share God's love with others. Then, with the authority Jesus gives His followers, I rebuked the evil spirit that disturbed Seng each night, commanding it to cease its harassment completely.

Most importantly, I claimed the blood of Jesus to break any authority the demon believed it had over this child. Throughout this, Seng slept peacefully, unaware of the spiritual battle being waged on his behalf.

Why would a demon have the authority to torment a child raised in a loving Christian home?

That night, for the first time in months, the ten o'clock hour passed without incident. Seng slept through until morning and, to my knowledge, has continued to sleep soundly every night since.

The case raises a profound question: Why would a demon have the authority to torment a child raised in a loving Christian home? While I don't have definitive answers, experience suggests that a generational spirit attachment in Seng's ancestry may have been the cause. Such spirits often claim access to families until that right is specifically canceled through the blood of Jesus.

Scripture reveals that God visits "the iniquity of the fathers upon the children to the third and fourth generations" (Exod. 20:5), not because He is vindictive, but because spiritual patterns and vulnerabilities can be passed down through families. The good news is that Jesus' sacrifice provides complete liberation from these generational patterns when we specifically invoke His blood to cancel ancestral spiritual claims.

Seng's deliverance illustrates key principles about spiritual warfare, particularly regarding children. First, the timing and consistency of his nighttime terrors—occurring at precisely the same hour—suggested supernatural involvement rather than normal childhood fears. Second, the immediate and complete cessation of these episodes after authoritative prayer indicates that the root cause was indeed spiritual. Finally, the specific invocation of Jesus' blood to break any demonic authority proved decisive in securing Seng's freedom.

God loves His people profoundly and desires the best for them. He suffers alongside us in our struggles. The spiritual battle for human souls operates according to rules of engagement, with God typically working through human agents who don the armor of God and rely on His strength to combat unseen foes.

Jesus empowered His disciples to heal the sick, raise the dead, and cast out evil spirits, just as He himself did. Before ascending to heaven, He commissioned them with the words, "As the Father has sent Me, I also send you" (John 20:2). This same authority extends to believers today who walk closely with Christ.

What might happen if more Christian parents understood the spiritual dimensions of their children's unexplained fears or behaviors? How many children might be freed from torment if we recognized spiritual warfare for what it is, rather than attributing everything to psychology or normal development?

Seng's story reminds us that even the youngest and most innocent among us can become targets in the cosmic conflict—and that Jesus stands ready to defend them when we invoke His authority and apply His blood to break any claims of darkness.

Multiple Reasons for Harassment

I regarded them as the cream of Australian Christian youth—twelve students who had dedicated a year of their lives to learning more about God and sharing their knowledge with others. I was honored to conduct a seminar on demon possession and deliverance at their training school.

Hour after hour, their interest never waned as I shared the stories you've been reading. These bright young people asked thoughtful questions and engaged deeply with the theological implications of spiritual warfare. By every measure, the seminar was a tremendous success.

But at the end, I issued an invitation that revealed the shocking truth about demonic infiltration in Christian communities: "If you feel demons are harassing you, please speak with me privately."

Three of these exemplary young believers asked for confidential meetings.

The first was a Caucasian young man whose life was being traumatized by demonic attacks. As we discussed the source of his torment, he identified computer games as the primary culprit. Before joining the school, he had been addicted to playing *Dungeons and Dragons* and similar games that he now recognized as doorways to spiritual harassment.

Although he had deleted the games from his computer, the demons hadn't deleted themselves from his life. Together, we prayed for forgiveness and victory over his addiction, claiming Christ's blood to cancel the spiritual rights his gaming habits had granted to evil forces.

The second student was a young woman of Indian descent whose family had emigrated from India to Australia. She described terrifying experiences in her bedroom—objects being thrown around, her bed shaking violently—that left her exhausted and afraid.

When I asked for her thoughts about the source of these attacks, she revealed that her great-grandfather had been a spirit priest. As the firstborn of her generation, she was next in line to inherit this spiritual legacy and its associated supernatural powers.

As a committed Christian, she rejected this demonic inheritance, but the generational spirits weren't accepting her refusal quietly. The constant harassment was designed to wear down her resistance until she submitted to her "destiny" as the family's next spirit medium.

We prayed together, confessing her ancestors' sins and claiming Jesus' blood to break the generational spirits' authority over her family line.

The third young man was from the Congo, having emigrated to Australia after years in a refugee camp. During his teenage years, he had witnessed horrific violence and death that left him with severe mental trauma. Demons were exploiting these wounds by forcing him to relive the traumatic scenes through constant flashbacks and nightmares.

We sought mental and emotional healing from Jesus while claiming Christ's blood to cancel the demons' rights to torment him based on his traumatic experiences.

Three different students. Three completely different entry points for demonic harassment: entertainment addiction, generational spirits, and trauma exploitation. Together, their cases revealed the sophisticated nature of Satan's strategy against believers.

Computer games represent one of the enemy's most successful modern deceptions. While some are openly demonic and others are simply violent, even seemingly innocent games can become idols that distract players from God while creating addictive patterns that demons can exploit. I've watched academically strong students decline rapidly after acquiring smartphones and becoming game addicts—arriving late for class, sleeping through lessons, and prioritizing virtual achievements over genuine spiritual growth.

Generational spirits represent the enemy's long-term investment strategy, claiming ownership of family lines through ancestral involvement in occult practices. Many Christians, particularly those of African or Asian descent, discover that deceased relatives were traditional healers or spirit priests whose spiritual agreements still affect subsequent generations.

Trauma exploitation reveals demons as opportunistic predators who take advantage of wounds inflicted by others. Whether the violence is real or dramatized through movies and books, evil spirits can use exposure to brutality as doorways for harassment through fear, nightmares, and psychological torment.

What shocked me most about these three cases was their context: these attacks were occurring among some of the most committed young Christians I had ever encountered. If demons could harass students in a Seventh-day Adventist training school—young people who had sacrificed a year of their lives for Christian education and service—what was happening in ordinary churches where spiritual warfare awareness was minimal?

The answer was sobering: Satan's infiltration of Christian communities was far more extensive than most believers realized. Entertainment, ancestry, and trauma were just three of many doorways through which demons could gain access to believers' lives.

But these cases also revealed hope: when Christians understood the sources of their harassment and cooperated with God in closing spiritual doors, freedom was possible. Each of these three students found relief through confession, renunciation, and claiming Christ's authority over the specific areas where demons had gained access.

Their stories forced me to confront uncomfortable questions about the state of modern Christianity: How many believers were struggling with spiritual harassment without understanding its source? How many churches were addressing symptoms while missing the spiritual warfare component entirely? How many families were passing down spiritual bondage from generation to generation without realizing the pattern?

Most importantly, how many people could find freedom if they simply understood the biblical principles of spiritual warfare and applied them to their specific situations?

Typhoid, Not Demons

Sometimes the most important deliverance is admitting you're fighting the wrong battle.

Ong had been a model church member for years. He faithfully attended church services from the time he was baptized into Christ Jesus and became a member of the Seventh-day Adventist Church. Then, seemingly overnight, he transformed into someone his family didn't recognize. Violent outbursts replaced gentle conversation. Irrational behavior destroyed his reputation for stability.

The call had come urgently from the Siem Reap City church: "Come quickly. Ong needs deliverance from demons."

The symptoms of demon possession fit Ong's case. People noticed a sudden behavioral transformation in Ong, uncontrollable anger, and actions contrary to his established character. Every indicator suggested we were dealing with possession by an evil spirit.

For days, our prayer team surrounded Ong with intercession and commands. "In the name of Jesus, leave him!" we repeatedly commanded. But unlike every other deliverance I had witnessed, nothing happened. No demons manifested, no spirits departed, and no relief came to this tormented young man.

The spiritual warfare playbook that had never failed me was producing zero results.

Then I learned about typhoid.

Buried in conversations about Ong's recent medical history was a crucial detail: he had just recovered from a severe case of typhoid fever. As I researched the aftermath of this disease, a troubling possibility emerged. In rare cases, typhoid could cause lingering psychiatric symptoms that mimicked demonic possession almost perfectly.

What if we were commanding demons that weren't there? What if we were fighting a spiritual battle against a medical condition that required medical intervention instead of supernatural deliverance? We decided to take Ong to the psychiatric ward.

Within weeks of starting psychiatric medication, Ong's symptoms began to diminish. The violent outbursts decreased. The irrational behavior subsided. Gradually, the gentle church member we had known for years reemerged from behind the medical crisis that had hidden him.

When Ong later stopped taking his medication briefly, the disturbing symptoms returned, confirming that his condition was medical, not spiritual. He now understands that maintaining his normal life requires daily medication.

This case became one of my most important teachers about the complexity of human suffering. Not every unusual behavior signals demonic activity, and not every crisis requires spiritual warfare. Sometimes, the most loving thing we can do is recognize the limits of our spiritual tools and seek help from medical professionals.

But how do we know the difference? When should we pray for deliverance, and when should we prescribe medication? When does faith become presumption, and when does medical treatment become avoidance of spiritual reality?

The answers require the very gift we most desperately need in spiritual warfare: divine discernment from the Holy Spirit. God's wisdom must guide us through the complex intersection of medical and spiritual realities. We must be willing to admit when our spiritual diagnosis might be wrong and remain open to God working through doctors as well as deliverance practitioners.

Ong's story taught me that true spiritual warfare sometimes means including medical solutions. The enemy can win if we approach a problem with the wrong tools, whether we're using medical solutions for spiritual problems or spiritual solutions for medical problems.

The goal isn't to prove our spiritual authority—it's to bring genuine healing to suffering people. Sometimes, that healing comes through commanding demons to leave, and sometimes, it comes through helping people find the proper medication. Wisdom lies in knowing which approach serves God's purposes and the person's well-being.

CHAPTER 10:
The Cost of Ministry

Sexual Temptation: A Satanic Strategy

"Can I be your daughter?"

The young girl's question seemed innocent enough as she approached me while I knelt in the hot sun, digging post holes for a fence around our newly purchased property. But what happened next revealed it was anything but innocent.

The year was 1996, and God had called my wife, Wendy, and me to a significant mission that would impact His kingdom in Cambodia. After fourteen years of happy marriage and raising two children together, we had purchased forty-seven acres (nineteen hectares) of land about three miles (five kilometers) outside Siem Reap City to develop a church and training center for church planters and Bible workers.

The fence was our first priority before we constructed the buildings. For days, I had been alone on the property, digging holes in sandy soil for wooden fence posts. That's when Champa, a plump sixteen-year-old girl from the nearby village, approached with her unusual request.

Champa, a girl from the nearby village, approached with her unusual request.

What transpired in my mind upon her arrival was even more unusual. I immediately felt an overwhelming sexual desire for this girl. This sensation was out of character for me. What's more, I did not find her physically attractive at all, yet suddenly I found myself battling intense temptation toward this teenager.

With shocking clarity, I realized I was under direct satanic attack. Satan knew that if he could tempt me into sexual sin with this minor, he would effectively destroy our God-given project before it even began. If Satan could get me to sin in this way, it would not only devastate my family but would undermine the entire ministry before the first building was finished.

> ## I was under direct satanic attack.

Day after day, Champa returned to linger near the fence line. The intense temptation continued to harass me like a physical presence. I spent my work hours in constant prayer, desperately seeking God's protection and strength. "Lord, this isn't me," I prayed repeatedly. "Shield my mind and heart so I will not fail You."

Looking back, I recognize that I should have discussed what was happening with Wendy, creating accountability and spiritual partnership in the battle. But shame and fear kept me silent, so I fought alone, relying entirely on God's strength. The spiritual assault continued for two weeks, with Champa even visiting our home in the city to meet my family—Satan pressing his advantage at every opportunity.

After two weeks of continuous prayer and resistance, something remarkable happened: the oppressive temptation vanished completely. Where intense desire had been, there was nothing but appropriate paternal concern for a young woman I might help spiritually. God had granted victory as I continually sought His presence. After this, Champa stopped coming around.

Later, I learned that Champa's mother was a spirit medium—a detail that added significance to the attack. (I share Champa's mother's story in Chapter 6, "Smoked Baby Talks.") More tellingly, Champa herself had become a prostitute, suggesting the evil spiritual forces behind our encounter had other plans for her life when their strategy with me failed.

About a year later, Champa reappeared at our church in Siem Reap City. This time, she approached the Khmer pastor and me with a very different request: she needed help to cast out an evil spirit. She had recently married and believed she was possessed. Given our previous encounter, I had no trouble believing her claim. The pastor and I prayed together for her, commanding the evil spirit to leave. Champa left our small church feeling grateful. While she never officially joined the church, years later, she sent her children to our Christian school—perhaps the one positive outcome of our connection.

Throughout my forty years in mission service, I've witnessed many missionaries face similar targeted attacks. Some emerged victorious; others did not. The pattern is clear: the greater God's calling on a person's life, the more intensely Satan attempts to undermine that ministry. Sexual temptation is a particularly effective weapon in his arsenal, but it's just one of many. Sickness, death, loss of property, team conflicts—all can be strategically deployed to derail God's work.

Whatever strategy the enemy uses, we must stand firm in God's principles and honor Him by achieving victory. Peter's warning remains urgently relevant: "Be sober, be vigilant; because your adversary the devil walks about like a roaring lion, seeking whom he may devour" (1 Peter 5:8).

As a child of God, I'm profoundly grateful for Scripture's promises that have given me courage and strength when attacks come:

"No temptation has overtaken you except such as is common to man; but God is faithful, who will not allow you to be tempted beyond what you are able, but with the temptation will also make the way of escape, that you may be able to bear it" (1 Cor. 10:13).

"Casting down arguments and every high thing that exalts itself against the knowledge of God, bringing every thought into captivity to the obedience of Christ" (2 Cor. 10:5).

My journey toward victory over temptation is anchored in Christ's promise: "I can do all things through Christ who strengthens me" (Phil. 4:13). "You are of God, little children, and have overcome them, because He who is in you is greater than he who is in the world" (1 John 4:4).

Each day, I choose to affirm with Paul: "I have been crucified with Christ; it is no longer I who live, but Christ lives in me; and the life which I now live in the flesh I live by faith in the Son of God, who loved me and gave Himself for me" (Gal. 2:20).

The battle against Champa's strange allure wasn't primarily about sexual temptation—it was about Satan's desperate attempt to prevent a ministry that would eventually lead hundreds of Cambodians to Christ. When we understand that our personal struggles often have kingdom significance, we fight with greater determination and purpose. My experience with this targeted spiritual attack ultimately strengthened my resolve and dependence on God, preparing me for the greater challenges that would come in establishing the SALT Center.

What areas of vulnerability might Satan be targeting in your life or ministry? And how might viewing these struggles as spiritual warfare rather than merely personal challenges change your approach to overcoming them?

Attacked Personally

The pain struck without warning, draining my strength as if someone had pulled a plug in my soul.

My students and I had committed to a twenty-four-hour fast while working with a victim of demon possession. The day began normally with worship, followed by prayer in our classroom for the one in need of deliverance. Then local villagers carried in an unconscious man, transporting him in a hammock tied to a pole.

I divided my students into two teams, each ministering to a different demonized patient. The spiritual atmosphere was intense but manageable—until the demons decided to strike back at the leader.

Every ounce of energy suddenly drained from my body. Pain wracked every muscle and join. The message was clear: the spirits were punishing me for leading these deliverance teams, hoping that attacking the commander would scatter the troops.

Unable to continue ministering, I instructed my students to persist until both victims were free, then mounted my motorcycle for the short ride home. The normally simple one-third mile (500-meter) journey became a struggle against weakness and pain, making it difficult to drive in a straight line.

Once home, I lay down on a thin mattress and spent the rest of the day in agony, praising God.

You might wonder why I was thanking the very God who seemed to have failed as my shield and protector. Hadn't David declared in 2 Samuel 22:2–4 (NIV), "The Lord is my rock, my fortress and my deliverer; my God is my rock, in whom I take refuge, my shield and the horn of my salvation. He is my stronghold, my refuge and my savior—from violent people you save me. I called to the Lord, who is worthy of praise, and have been saved from my enemies."

Where was my divine protection when I needed it most?

But my perspective was different. I had voluntarily joined God in a battle to rescue souls from Satan's grip. If my heavenly Father wanted to bring honor to Himself by allowing me to be tested like Job, I could accept that assignment. My choice was simple: grumble and complain, giving Satan a victory, or spend the painful day rejoicing in God's goodness regardless of circumstances.

The students' practical experience in deliverance without their teacher brought freedom to both patients while strengthening their faith in God's power. They also gained confidence to minister similarly when they returned to their home villages—an outcome that might not have occurred if I had been present to do everything for them.

As evening approached, I decided it was time to bathe at our outdoor well. Dragging my pain-ridden body to the well, I slowly pulled up a bucket of water and poured it over my head.

Something miraculous happened. The pain vanished instantly from each area touched by the water. Simultaneously, strength returned to those body parts. By the time I was completely wet, I was pain free and strong again.

My praise for God reached new levels. I don't know what transpired in the spiritual realm, but I imagined God saying to Satan, "I win. You lose," just as He must have done when Job's test was completed and his fortunes were restored.

This experience taught me profound lessons about the true nature of spiritual warfare. Deliverance practitioners may face attacks not due to sin in their lives, but precisely because they're cooperating with God to set captives free from Satan's influence. The more effective our ministry, the more likely we are to experience retaliation.

But these attacks also serve divine purposes beyond our immediate understanding. My day of pain while my students succeeded without me taught them that God's power didn't depend on human leaders. They learned to rely directly on divine authority rather than looking to their teacher as the source of supernatural intervention.

The timing of my healing—instant restoration when I chose to wash— reminded me that God's protection is real, even when He temporarily allows testing. Like Job, I was being observed by spiritual intelligences who needed to see whether God's servants would remain faithful when divine protection seemed to fail.

Most importantly, this experience prepared me for the humility I would need in future cases where demons didn't immediately bow to Jesus' authority. Having been personally attacked and then dramatically healed, I could trust God's sovereignty even when His methods seemed inconsistent with my expectations.

The battle for souls requires soldiers willing to face personal risk for the sake of others' freedom. If we only minister when we're guaranteed protection from all opposition, we'll never engage the enemy where the fighting is fiercest and the need is greatest.

Don't Read That Book!

The attacks began as soon as my students opened the book.

In 2024, I published my first book, *When Sacrifice is Gain*. The book shares stories from forty years of mission work and the lessons God has taught us along the way. It illustrates living the faith of Jesus and includes some of the deliverance stories found here. Our story has profoundly impacted many people, but there is a darker side to reading the book.

Recently, I began hearing reports of demonic attacks on our students when they started reading *When Sacrifice is Gain*. Four girls in the senior class began to feel oppressed, some experiencing difficulty breathing while reading it. Three of the girls decided to stop reading, and the oppression ceased. The fourth girl persisted despite the demonic oppression, rebuking the demons instead.

An eighth-grade student named Sreyka came to ask for prayer. She had started reading *When Sacrifice is Gain* and began experiencing attacks. She heard what sounded like the voice of her deceased grandfather telling her not to read the book. The oppression caused Sreyka to have two sleepless nights.

Although Sreyka is only in grade eight, she is an active missionary for God. She records messages in our media center, teaches a children's Sabbath school class, addresses high school assemblies about God's love, and tells children's stories during church services. She prays often and reads her Bible daily for personal devotions. This student is humble, kind, and Christlike.

To Sreyka's knowledge, nothing has happened that would grant demons access. Yet one night, an evil spirit oppressed her, and the oppression escalated to possession. The spirit loudly proclaimed, "Do not read the book."

Female students and their deans gathered around Sreyka in the dorm room, praying for her and singing hymns. The demon continued repeating the same phrases. I arrived about half an hour after this began. Although I ordered the spirit to leave in the name of Jesus, it ignored me and kept shouting. For the next hour we prayed, read the Bible aloud—which the demon clearly disliked. We sang hymns, and commanded the evil spirit to leave.

As the demon's intensity began to wane, I asked Sreyka to call out the name of Jesus and request His help. After several attempts, she managed to mouth the name "Jesus." We encouraged her to keep trying until she could say aloud, "Jesus, help me." At that point, she regained control of her mind and voice, but her hands twisted and moved like a Khmer dancer, indicating that the demon had not yet departed. I continued to command the spirit to leave until it finally did.

She described that it had felt like two entities were in her body, with one preventing her from speaking. As she tried to call on the name of Jesus, the demon's power weakened until she could vocalize again, at which point the demon retreated. James writes, "Resist the devil and he will flee from you" (James 4:7). We praised God for evicting the evil spirit and prayed with Sreyka, claiming the blood of Jesus to revoke any further rights the demons might have to enter her. Sreyka slept well through the night and faced no trouble the next day despite continuing to read *When Sacrifice is Gain*.

Questions arise from cases like this. For example, why would a young woman with a good relationship with God become possessed? I do not have the answer to this question, nor do others. What I do know is to trust God, even when I do not have all the answers.

When Sacrifice is Gain is having a profoundly positive impact on our students, and these demonic attacks appear to be efforts to discourage reading it. Ironically, the opposite has occurred. As the young women shared their experiences, more and more students asked if they could have a copy of the book.

While the above stories unfolded, Pastor Victor Bejota,[4] his family, and a team of Brazilian missionaries were working with our media team to increase engagement with the videos they had produced. After they returned to their

4   Although most names in the book have been changed, I have permission to use Pastor Victor's actual name.

base in Thailand, Pastor Victor began reading *When Sacrifice is Gain.* Below is text from our chat sessions after he started reading the book.

[10 Feb. 2025, 10:07:36] Victor Bejota:

Regarding the book, it's been really powerful. Once I start reading it, I can't stop—it's been incredibly inspiring. But I must confess that some strange things have started happening here, and I'm not sure if it's related to that. My youngest daughter had a minor accident yesterday that left a scratch on her leg. After that, she hasn't been able to walk. She doesn't feel any pain in the area, and when we press it, she feels nothing; she just doesn't have the strength in her legs to walk. I'm on my way to the hospital now to see what's going on, but honestly, it wouldn't surprise me if I find out nothing is physically wrong and that it could be something spiritual happening. But we know that our God is more powerful and that things like this show us that we are on the right path, so we will keep going!

[10 Feb. 2025, 10:07:43] Victor Bejota:

Yesterday, I spoke with a Cambodian, which helped me understand the spiritual dimension present in Siem Reap. I was unaware that the Angkor Wat temple serves as such a powerful spiritual center. After hearing the stories, I realized why God has been prompting us to focus on spiritual warfare— because it appears to be more intense and evident in this region.

[11 Feb. 2025, 07:57:29] Tim Maddocks:

What's the latest on your daughter's leg?

[11 Feb. 2025, 08:02:58] Victor Bejota:

She still can't walk. We didn't go to the hospital yesterday, but we plan to go today. She isn't in pain; we touched her leg and she didn't feel anything hurt, but she still can't walk... We will go to the hospital today.

[11 Feb. 2025, 11:11:12] Tim Maddocks:

It sounds like a demonic attack.

[11 Feb. 2025, 11:12:48] Victor Bejota:

Do you recommend anything? We will intensify our prayers for her and ask more people to pray with us.

[11 Feb. 2025, 11:14:45] Tim Maddocks:

Consider calling the elders together to anoint her. At the same time, rebuke the demon of paralysis that may be preventing her from walking. This situation doesn't seem to be possession but rather harassment.

[11 Feb. 2025, 11:16:11] Victor Bejota:

I will do that.

[11 Feb. 2025, 11:27:33] Victor Bejota:

We just did an x-ray, and the doctor said everything is normal.

[13 Feb. 2025, 06:47:32] Victor Bejota:

My daughter has started walking.

[13 Feb. 2025, 06:48:38] Victor Bejota:

I called the elders to come pray for her, and she began walking just ten minutes before they arrived. I believe Satan was trying to embarrass me in front of the elders. We visited another hospital yesterday, and the doctors confirmed that everything is okay.

A few weeks later Victor filled in more details for me.

[4 Mar. 2025, 06:28:01] Victor Bejota:

I wanted to share some updates....

He went on to tell me more about his daughter's healing. He had learned of earnest prayers that had gone up for the girl even before the elders arrived; these had been answered.

He also shared that the challenges weren't over. His daughter got four fingers shut in the car door; she'd swallowed a coin and nearly choked; a scorpion was found crawling on her. A fellow missionary was facing attacks. Newly appointed ministry leaders were in a serious motorcycle crash, hit by a drunk.

He summarized with these words, "The struggles have been intense, but the deliverance has been even greater. This only confirms that we are on the right path." Minutes later he added some closing thoughts.

[4 Mar. 2025, 06:31:59] Victor Bejota:

Our time with you deeply impacted everyone in our group, especially the example of faith that you and Wendy have shown. It has left a lasting impression on us.

Since our return, we've been reading your book daily. Many challenges we've faced occurred at the exact moment I was reading it. One night, while reading, my father came to my window to inform me that Cintia had just been in a motorcycle accident.

I know this isn't a coincidence.

We continue to read your book daily—some stories I have read three times already. We're reading it together with our missionaries, and last Sabbath, I even shared it with our church because we have been so blessed by your testimony and journey.

Thank you for your impact on us.

We have become bolder in our mission, praying with greater courage and truly learning what it means to sacrifice for the cause. Our new motto has become:

"Go anywhere. Do anything. For as long as it takes. No matter the cost."

We are striving to inspire more people with this vision.

Your willingness to let the Holy Spirit lead you has motivated us to be more attentive to His voice. We are learning to relinquish our own agendas and ask God to take full control of our days. This has already begun to yield incredible results.

———❦———

The dialogue above illustrates the very real battles God's people are experiencing today. Satan and his demonic forces will do anything—to the extent God allows—to discourage His faithful followers. The biblical story of Job offers a glimpse into the spiritual dimension, helping us understand why God's children on this earth, like Pastor Victor's little daughter, experience attacks from demons. When God's people remain faithful amid the trials imposed by Satan and his forces, God is honored, and Satan is defeated.

As a child of God, our role is to trust Him as Job did even when His promise to be our shield seems to falter. Jesus, the pure and holy Son of God, also faced demonic attacks during His time on earth. He rebuked Satan and bravely continued His mission—a mission that He passed on to us, His disciples (see John 20:21). No matter what Satan does to hinder or discourage us, we are called to continue the mission of rescuing those trapped in the darkness of his kingdom with the same courage and faith Jesus demonstrated.

SECTION FIVE:

MATURE UNDERSTANDING:
Understanding Tragic Outcomes

CHAPTER 11:
When Deliverance Doesn't Come

Zero Day

I had never encountered a problem like this before. Her neighbor brought Sokun from the third village to the west, seeking help. From what the two women told me, Sokun's husband had never abused her. Her children seemed happy and normal. She appeared to be in good health and had no history of mental illness or recent sickness. Sokun was fully functional mentally and physically—yet she claimed to never have married or had children. She complained that living in a home with a man and children that were not hers was very difficult. Her husband and children had no idea what had happened Sokun's memory.

Sokun was a Buddhist and lived near the local Buddhist temple. The average Cambodian Buddhist occasionally visits the temple for ceremonies that may involve worshiping the Buddha. Most worship, however, occurs at home and focuses on appeasing the spirits of their ancestors or the spirits believed to inhabit the land. These practices can create openings for demonic possession, though there seems to be no predictable pattern for when possession occurs.

In Sokun's case, we could not identify a specific reason for her possession, but due to the sudden and unusual social changes she experienced, we assumed demonic influence was at the root of her problem.

We asked God to intervene in Sokun's life and commanded the evil spirits to leave her. God's power through prayer for Sokun returned her to her previous self. She acknowledged her marriage and her children. She returned to her family and chose to start attending the local Seventh-day Adventist church.

For several months, Sokun attended church regularly, slowly learning about Jesus and His promise of eternal life. Then she allowed herself to become busy on Sabbaths and stopped attending. After several weeks, the demons returned. This time Sokun came alone, with a sad story to share.

> *Sokun told me that the demons had informed her that her sins were now too many for God to forgive.*

Sokun told me that the demons had informed her that her sins were now too many for God to forgive. I opened the Bible and shared verse after verse to show her that what the demons told her was not true. She listened to the verses but insisted that they applied to others, not to her. She also spoke about her "zero day." Unable to understand what she meant, I continued to use the Word of God to convince her that she had been deceived about God's character. She remained adamant that God could not forgive her this time. Before she left, I asked her to return to church the following Sabbath and invite her husband and children to come with her. Sokun agreed and departed.

She returned home and told her husband about my request, and he agreed to accompany her and the children to church the next Sabbath. However, when Sabbath morning arrived, Sokun left the house and did not return. Her husband assumed she had gone to buy eggs for breakfast, but when she failed to come back, he went out looking for her. He found Sokun behind the house, hanging from a tree. That Sabbath became her zero day—the day the demons told her she must die because her sins were too many for God to forgive. Demons can be very persuasive, whispering thoughts into a person's mind in a way that leads them to believe the thoughts are their own.

Sokun's cremation was unlike the usual ceremonies. As her body burned, fear pervaded the assembly. The demons responsible for her suicide were thought to be released in the smoke and attendees believed those demons would enter anyone who happened to inhale it.

I did not share their fear, but I couldn't help but wonder—if our local Bible worker or I had spent more time teaching Sokun and her family after her deliverance, perhaps this story would have had a different ending. It is too easy to assume that once someone has been set free from demons and is attending church, everything will be fine. The Cambodian people, like many others, are steeped in traditions and superstitions that shape their understanding of the supernatural. While they have a better grasp of the supernatural than a post-modern person, their understanding differs significantly from the biblical perspective. Teaching a biblical worldview takes time, but it is a worthwhile investment if it leads to eternal life for the learner.

Her story haunted me with questions that had no easy answers: How do we protect newly delivered people from spiritual deception? How do we teach biblical worldview to those steeped in superstition and tradition? How do we ensure that freedom from demons leads to lasting transformation instead of temporary relief?

Most troubling of all: How many others were listening to similar lies, believing that their sins were too great for God's mercy, contemplating zero days of their own?

Black Magic Took His Life

Nigel stood motionless in his grandfather's house, balanced on one leg like a strange human statue. Cigarette smoke curled around his expressionless face as his empty eyes stared into nothingness. What had reduced this teenager to this bizarre state? And why did he speak only on Buddhist holy days?

The answer lay in a fateful decision made weeks earlier. Nigel lived with his elderly grandfather in a village some distance from our SALT Center. Desperate for power Nigel visited a family known for practicing black magic. The paraphernalia on display had fascinated him—objects of supposed power that promised control in a life where perhaps he felt he had none.

Nigel did not seem to understand that the family had been seeking escape from the demons they served. They knew the evil spirits would exact vengeance if they simply abandoned their demonic objects. Seeing an opportunity for a "legal" transfer of their spiritual burden, they offered Nigel the items and the power they contained. For a young man seeking significance, the offer proved irresistible.

His grandfather, recognizing the danger, had demanded Nigel return the items. But when Nigel arrived at the family's home, he found it locked. Leaving the items on the doorstep seemed reasonable. When the family returned, however, the husband urinated on the items—a deliberate act of rejection that transferred the spiritual attachment back to Nigel. That same afternoon, Nigel went insane.

"How long has he been like this?" I asked Nigel's Aunt Ming. She lived in the same village as Nigel, but she had recently given her life to Jesus and become a Seventh-day Adventist. She was studying at the SALT Center to learn how to share her newfound faith in Jesus. She shared her nephew's story after my spiritual warfare class. Ming's eyes reflected both love for her nephew and desperation for help. "He stands like that all day. Only speaks sometimes on holy days. We don't know what to do."

The students and I developed a plan. We would fast and pray for Nigel, then go to the village to bring him and his grandfather to the SALT Center, where we could pray for his deliverance and teach him about Jesus. We agreed to keep our plan private, believing our plans would be more effective if villagers weren't alerted. However, as we walked through the rice fields toward Nigel's home, the villagers we passed startled us with an unexpected greeting.

"You've finally come for Nigel," one said. "We've been expecting you."

The students exchanged confused glances. "How did you know we were coming?" they asked.

"During the last Buddhist holy day, Nigel was shouting all through the village that students from the SALT Center would come for him."

A chill ran through me. "What is spoken, demons hear," I explained to the students. Though they cannot read our thoughts, demonic forces hear our audible communications—a sobering reminder of the spiritual battle's reality.

When we arrived, Nigel's grandfather welcomed us, his weathered face a map of suffering. Nigel stood in the corner, one leg raised, his vacant eyes briefly flickering with recognition—or was it fear?

What followed was not the dramatic deliverance I had hoped for but rather a marathon of spiritual persistence. Nigel and his grandfather came to the SALT Center, where we prayed for him and commanded the demon to leave, but nothing changed. Days passed. Then weeks. The students cared for Nigel tirelessly, providing food, helping him shower, and showing him Jesus' love in practical ways. We fasted again and prayed, yet Nigel remained trapped in his silent prison, standing on one leg, now without cigarettes, which we don't allow at the Center.

In three months, he spoke only once—when he angrily threw his plate across the room with a short, unintelligible outburst.

As our four-month training program drew to a close, we held one final day of fasting and prayer for Nigel. When this, too, yielded no change, I knelt before him, looking directly into his vacant eyes.

"Nigel," I said gently, extending my hand, "if you want Jesus to help you, take my hand."

Without hesitation, Nigel tucked both hands firmly behind his back. The message was unmistakable: he had chosen to remain with the darkness that possessed him.

> *Without hesitation, Nigel tucked both hands firmly behind his back. The message was unmistakable.*

What was at stake here wasn't just Nigel's mental state or social functioning—it was his eternal destiny. Yet Jesus, who respects human choice, would not override Nigel's decision. The students and I had done everything in our power to create an opportunity for deliverance, but the final choice had to be Nigel's.

Six months after returning home, Nigel died. He was never delivered from the enslavement and torture of evil spirits. Nigel's decision to trust Satan became final at Nigel's death because "it is appointed for men to die once, but after this the judgment" (Heb. 9:27). What promises did the lying spirits make to keep Nigel trusting? Or did they threaten Him? When I think of the torture and lies Satan's spirits kept Nigel under, it reminds me of why God will destroy them forever. They are vicious liars without empathy. They are filled with hatred, and they are terribly dangerous to those who do not flee to Jesus in faith. Nigel's story is a profound reminder that spiritual freedom is offered to all, but it must be accepted. Jesus stands at the door and knocks, but He will not break it down when we lock Him out. We must choose to open the door.

Demons Defile Our Character

I had been doing deliverance ministry for years, learning to recognize the obvious spirits—demons of pride, cursing, false tongues, abandonment. But as I studied how evil forces operated in believers' lives, something bigger began to emerge. Maybe the battle for human character was far more extensive than any of us realized.

Here's what I learned: demons defile us through sin, and sin can be overcome. God's power is so strong that Christians who persist in trusting and following the Holy Spirit can grow into total victory over sin.

Here's the first truth that revolutionized my understanding: **Sin is an empty lie that has nothing at all to desire.**

Sin itself is deception because it promises good but delivers misery. Demons tell us they'll make us powerful or happy, but they give us the misery of a hunger that's never satisfied. They entice people with promises of pleasure, then take away true pleasure and give self-loathing, pain, and death instead. Sin corrodes character like acid corrodes the body. Sin takes away our ability to find joy in other people's joy, to feel gratitude, kindness, empathy, and love. Ask the Holy Spirit to reveal to you how worthless sin is, and He will.

This brings me to the second truth that transformed my life: **God withholds nothing good from us and forbids only those things that bring damage and death.** When demons put the temptation in your mind that God asks you to give up something good, remember two things: First, God only asks you to give up things that will cause you misery. Second, God owns everything good, and He intends to give it all to us throughout eternity. The Bible puts it simply: "No good thing will God withhold from those who walk uprightly" (Psalm 84:11).

Ellen White describes this truth beautifully: "God does not require us to give up anything that is for our best interest to retain. In all that He does, He has the well-being of His children in view. Would that all who have not chosen Christ might realize that He has something vastly better to offer them than they are seeking for themselves. Man is doing the greatest injury and injustice to his own soul when he thinks and acts contrary to the will of God. No real joy can be found in the path forbidden by Him who knows what is best and who plans for the good of His creatures. The path of transgression is the path of misery and destruction" (E. G. White, *Steps to Christ*, p. 46).

One more promise that helps right now: whatever you give up for God, He will give you a hundred times more in this life.

Jesus Himself makes you this promise: "Assuredly, I say to you, there is no one who has left house or brothers or sisters or father or mother or wife or children or lands, for My sake and the gospel's, who shall not receive a hundredfold now in this time—houses and brothers and sisters and mothers and children and lands, with persecutions—and in the age to come, eternal life" (Mark 10:29-30).

Doesn't it make more sense to trust the words of Jesus rather than the words of demons?

Demons defile our characters in ways we often don't recognize.

In the book of Revelation, Jesus makes a tremendous promise: "I will give of the fountain of the water of life freely to him who thirsts" (Revelation 21:6). Water represents cleansing, and that's exactly why Jesus died for us— so that with our permission and cooperation, He can cleanse us from all unrighteousness (1 John 1:9). That cleansing doesn't just include forgiving us for sins we've committed but also includes giving us victory over sinful habits and tendencies. Part of that victory comes from Him helping us break relationships we may have with the demons who encourage those habits.

Jesus goes on to say, "He who overcomes shall inherit all things, and I will be his God, and He shall be my son" (Revelation 21:7). Freedom from sin is God's goal for us because, together with Jesus, He wants us to inherit all things good. Even in our sinful state, we can imagine the joy God's way brings. Paul wrote, "Eye has not seen, nor ear heard, neither have entered into the heart of man, the things which God has prepared for them that love him, but God *has revealed them to us* through His Spirit" (1 Corinthians 2:9-10, emphasis added). It is true that physical eyes and physical ears have not seen and heard what we will see and hear in Heaven, but let's not stop there because the next verse says that through our spiritual senses, the Holy Spirit has revealed what is waiting for us. It's like the Holy Spirit is a university full of books with pictures and words that reveal to us what God has prepared. Don't focus on the flesh. Focus on the Spirit, and the worthless things of this world will grow strangely dim, and demons will lose their power because their lies will no longer entice you.

We are deceived when we enjoy the sinful pleasures that demons offer us because they offer us only lies. God is the only one offering anything of value. When we realize that God gives us all truly good pleasures in obedience and that demons offer only false promises, victory over sin starts looking much easier.

"Now is the time to entreat that souls shall not only hear the word of God, but without delay secure oil in their vessels with their lamps. That oil is the righteousness of Christ. It represents character, and character is not transferable. No man can secure it for another. Each must obtain for himself a character purified from every stain of sin" (E.G. White, *Testimonies to Ministers*, p. 233). "The eye-salve is that spiritual discernment which will enable you to see the wiles of Satan and shun them, to detect sin and abhor it, to see the truth and obey it" (E.G. White, *Testimonies for the Church*, vol. 5, p. 233).

Demons want to live in us so they can destroy us from the inside out. God wants to live in us so He can transform us from the inside out. That transformation comes as we trust God to give us His perfect love and holy nature. The Bible says, "He who says he abides in Him ought himself also to walk just as He walked" (1 John 2:6) and "Whoever abides in Him does not sin" (1 John 3:6). If we have God living in our lives, His presence makes it possible for us to live the same sinless life that Jesus lived when He was here on earth.

Paul wrote that "I die daily" (1 Corinthians 15:31) and that "it is no longer I that lives but Christ that lives in me" (Galatians 2:20). This should be our daily desire, because where Christ lives, demons cannot remain.

The demons and Satan, their commander, know about their coming destruction in the lake of fire. Knowing there's no escape for them, they actively pursue the destruction of people, hoping to make God suffer from the loss of His children. Jesus spoke of that destruction: "But the fearful, and unbelieving, and the abominable, and murderers, and whoremongers, and sorcerers, and idolaters, and all liars, shall have their part in the lake which burns with fire and brimstone: which is the second death" (Revelation 21:8).

It's not God's desire that we should be destroyed by fire, and for this reason, Jesus Himself died for our sins and sent us the Holy Spirit to be our helper. Jesus said, "However, when He, the Spirit of truth, has come, He will guide you into all truth" (John 16:13).

The Shocking Scope of Demonic Influence

As I studied this deeper, I began to compile a list of behaviors that demons are known to influence. What shocked me was how extensive the list became. I had to organize it into four categories, and even then, the scope was staggering.

I encourage you to pray through this list, asking the Holy Spirit to show you if demons are influencing you in any of these behaviors. When the Holy Spirit reveals a problem behavior, confess the sin and claim the blood of Jesus to break any authority that any demon has on your life.[5] It sounds too easy, but Jesus' agonizing death on the cross has made it easy.

---

5 A useful deliverance manual, that includes questionnaires, is free for download from the website, www.SetFreeInChrist.org.

Behaviors, Circumstances, and Experiences Demons Love To Encourage and Take Advantage of:

1: Spiritual Abuse

Depravity - Demonic influence leading to moral corruption that separates one from God's holiness

False religion - Being deceived into following man-made spiritual systems that lead away from biblical truth

Folly - Demonic deception that causes rejection of divine wisdom in favor of worldly foolishness

Haters of God - Giving in to rebellious temptation to show active hostility toward the Creator

Heresies - Being deceived into teaching false doctrines that distort biblical truth and mislead others

Idolatry – Praying or bowing to statues; anything demons lead people to elevate above God in priority and devotion, for example, money, relationships, beauty, fame, self-deification

Ingratitude – Failing to recognize the contributions of others, especially God

Replacements for Christ – A subtle form of idolatry that replaces Christ's free gift with dead works, or anything that demons mislead a person to rely on for salvation other than Jesus

Sorcery - Seeking supernatural power apart from God through forbidden practices

Uncleanness - Moral and spiritual impurity that demons cultivate

Undiscerning - Lack of spiritual training or diligence that demons exploit to prevent wisdom in distinguishing truth from deception

Unholy revelries - Social pressures and peer influence that demons use to draw people into celebrations or "partying" that oppose God's standards and lead to debauchery

Unrighteousness - temptations that demons use to lead people away from God's moral standards

Witchcraft/Wicca – Similar to sorcery, but demons may disguise their power as magical forces of nature, or they lead people into the deception of "white magic"

Worldliness - Cultural values and social pressures that demons amplify to replace God's priorities with fallen world systems

2: Self Abuse

Alcohol use – Weakening mental and spiritual abilities with alcohol consumption

Anxiety - Circumstances and intrusive thoughts that demons use to steal trust in God's control

Bitterness – Real or illusory hurts and disappointments that demons amplify into resentment, poisoning one's heart and mind

Boredom - Tedious circumstances demons use to tempt people when God has better plans

Brokenness - Life defeats and trauma that demons exploit to keep people in spiritual and emotional despair or to encourage anger and hatred toward God

Obsessive work focus - Cultural expectations and personal insecurity that demons amplify into work idolatry destroying balance

Confusion - Demonic interference with identity and core beliefs that tempt people to reject God's order and gifts

Covetousness – A faithless focus on what others have, which demons use to create constant dissatisfaction and desire designed to damage trust in God's supply

Cutting - Emotional pain and trauma that demons redirect into physical self-harm as destructive coping

Denial - Demonic deception that prevents acknowledgment of obvious problems or destructive patterns

Depression - Life circumstances, and/or poor health, and demonic oppression that steal joy and hope

Despair - Overwhelming circumstances that demons magnify to destroy faith in God's promises

Disappointment - Unmet expectations that demons amplify into resentment and spiritual defeat

Discouragement - Life setbacks that demons magnify to destroy motivation and faith in God's goodness

Disgust - Difficult circumstances that demons exploit to create hatred toward life and self

Distraction - Demonic interference that prevents focus on what truly matters for spiritual growth

Excessive dieting - Cultural pressures and body image issues that demons amplify into dangerous obsession

Drug abuse - Using drugs as recreation or to numb spiritual pain resulting in corruption of mental clarity and faith, which open doors to demonic entrance

Envy – Bitter anger towards others' blessings and success that demons use to create resentment instead of gratitude and a focus away from God's plan and provision for your own life

Failure - Life setbacks or sins demons magnify to steal faith, hope and love

Destructive fantasy – When demons provide escape through deceptive imaginary worlds preventing engagement with reality or distorting perception to make lies seem true

Fear - Demonic intimidation and life circumstances that seek to overwhelm trust in God's protection and care

Forgetfulness - Human carelessness or Demonic interference with memory that affects important responsibilities and relationships

Futile thinking - Demonic influence on thought patterns that lead to failure and faithlessness

Obsessive gaming - Life stress and social difficulties that demons redirect into escapist virtual worlds, similar to vain imaginations

Gluttony - Emotional needs and stress that demons redirect toward destructive relationship with food

Greed - Natural desires for security that demons amplify into obsessive focus on wealth and possessions

Guilt - Past mistakes and failures that demons magnify to eclipse God's mercy and power

Hair pulling – Stress, anxiety, or obsession with appearance that demons redirect into compulsive self-damaging behaviors

Hatred - Real hurts and injustices that demons amplify into heart-poisoning anger and resentment

Heaviness - Life burdens and sorrows that demons magnify into loneliness and despair

Hypocrisy - Living a false double life

Ignorance - Limited opportunities or education that demons exploit to prevent growth and understanding

Impatience - Faithless demanding for immediate gratification

Inaptitude - Past failures or lack of confidence that demons magnify to prevent developing God-given abilities

Indecision - Demonic confusion and fear that creates paralysis when clear choices need to be made

Isolation - Pain, fear, or undesirability that demons exploit to prevent healthy relationships and community (This is why Jesus said invite those who cannot repay you to your dinners)

Jealousy – Others' relationships or achievements that demons use to create resentment and comparison

Laziness - Depression, discouragement, or past failures that demons amplify to prevent productive use of time

Loneliness - Circumstances of isolation that demons magnify while blocking awareness of God's presence and available relationships

Excessive money focus - Cultural values and personal insecurity that demons amplify into making wealth the measure of worth

Watching movies and television – Demons encourage people to watch shows that normalize ignoring God and accepting sin as harmless, that waste time, and decrease spiritual interests

Negativity - Difficult circumstances that demons exploit to create a hopeless focus on problems and darkness

Popularity obsession - Natural desire for acceptance that demons amplify into making others' approval the measure of self-worth or a singular focus they use to manipulate into sin

Pride – God-given talents or achievements that demons exploit to create belief in personal superiority and self-sufficiency they then use to entice someone into self-worship

Regrets - Past mistakes and missed opportunities that demons magnify to prevent embracing God's new mercies and plans to give a hopeful future

Rejection – Being denied acceptance, being hurt, feeling inadequate—demons use these experiences to entice people to seek deceptive answers that lead people to destruction

Restlessness - Demonic interference with inner peace that prevents experiencing the contentment God offers

Self-contempt - Past failures, criticism, and misunderstandings about God that demons magnify into despair or giving up on God

Selfish ambitions – Goals demons use to destroy empathy for others or interest in God's better plans

Shame - Real or false guilt demons use to blind a person from seeing Jesus and his power to forgive and transform

Excessive shopping - Emotional voids and identity issues that demons redirect toward finding fulfillment through purchases

Shyness - Uncertainty or natural temperament that demons exploit to prevent meaningful relationships and tempt people into deceptive groups or relationships with demons

Excessive silence – Withdrawal or vows of silence demons use to enter into a person's thoughts

Excessive slumber – Depression, life weariness or laziness demons use to snowball a person's life into despair, anxiety, or other states that prepare a person for their manipulation

Destructive social media use - Natural desire for connection that demons redirect into harmful comparison with others' edited lives

Sorrow - Real losses, grief that demons use to cause hopelessness or doubt in God

Sports obsession - Demons use sports obsessions to consume people's energies, money, time, focus, and spiritual interests.

Suicide - Overwhelming pain, hopelessness, or anger that demons use to block awareness of God's healing and hope, and to present suicide as a solution

Suspicion - Past betrayals that demons magnify into assuming the worst about others' motives and intentions

Tobacco use – Demons use various health-damaging addictions to manipulate people and weaken their bodies and minds

Unbelief - Difficult circumstances or false scientific theories demons use to create rejection of God's promises, power or existence.

Unforgiveness - Real hurts and offenses that demons magnify to prevent releasing pain and receiving God's healing

Unsound mind - Demonic interference with mental clarity allowing thoughts to become chaotic and destructive

Weariness - Life burdens and stress that demons amplify while blocking awareness of God's strength and rest available

3: Social Abuse

Abusive behavior - Personal pain or learned patterns that demons exploit into using power to harm and control others

Accusing - Personal insecurity, or a desire to manipulate or distract that demons use to tempt people to blame others with or without evidence

Aggression – Frustration, pain, or strength demons amplify beyond healthy limits into intimidation and destructive force

Ambushing - Attacking others when they are vulnerable or unprepared

Arguing - Insecurity and the need to be right that demons amplify into conflicts designed to win rather than understand and resolve

Arrogance - Success or compensation for insecurity that demons exploit into treating others as inferior

Backbiters - Giving in to the temptation to speak evil about others behind their backs

Blame – Merciless condemnation that fills a heart with darkness demons use to cover their entrance into a person's life

Boasting - constantly promoting oneself

Brutality - Giving into temptation to use excessive force or cruelty against others

Chattering - Nervousness or need for attention that demons exploit into talking excessively without considering others

Coarse joking - Humor that degrades and embarrasses others or makes light of sin

Coercion - Using pressure and manipulation to force others to act against their will

Conceited behavior - Success or deep insecurity that demons exploit into acting superior and dismissive

Condemning - Giving into temptation to judge others harshly without mercy or understanding

Contentions - Personal issues and unresolved pain that demons redirect into creating arguments and divisions

Control - Fear and insecurity that demons exploit into manipulating others to serve personal purposes

Cruelty - Giving into temptation to deliberately cause pain and suffering to others

Cursing - Giving into temptation to use words to tear down and harm others' spirits

Deceiving - Giving into temptation to lie to others for personal gain or to avoid consequences

Destructive criticism - Personal pain and insecurity that demons redirect into tearing others down instead of building up

Discord - Personal agendas and unresolved conflicts that demons use to create division in relationships

Disobedience - Giving into rebellious temptation to reject legitimate authority and structure

Disrespect - Personal pain or pride that demons exploit into treating others as if they have no value

Dissension - Stirring up division and conflict within groups for personal advantage

Distortion - Giving into temptation to twist others' words and actions to create false impressions

Division - Personal agendas that demons exploit to break apart unity and cooperation

Duplicity - Fear of consequences that demons exploit into being two-faced and dishonest in relationships

Egocentric behavior - Deep insecurity that demons mask by making everything about oneself at others' expense

Fault finding - Personal pain and insecurity that demons redirect into constantly seeking others' mistakes

Flattery - Using false praise manipulatively to gain personal advantage over others

Foolish talk - Lack of wisdom that demons exploit into speaking in ways that waste time and confuse

Forcefulness - Using excessive pressure to push others beyond reasonable limits for personal gain

Gaslighting - Manipulating others to question their own perception of reality for control

Gossiping - Giving into temptation to spread information about others that damages their reputation

Grumbling - Personal dissatisfaction that demons amplify into complaining in ways that discourage others

Harshness - Personal pain and frustration that demons redirect into treating others with unnecessary severity

Hostility - Personal pain and anger that demons amplify into approaching others with antagonism

Insults - Giving into temptation to use words specifically designed to hurt and demean others

Intimidation - Using fear tactics to control and manipulate others' behavior for personal advantage

Intolerance - Fear and prejudice that demons amplify into refusing to accept others who are different

Inventors of evil - Creating new ways to harm and corrupt others through malicious innovation

Judging - Giving into temptation to condemn others without mercy or understanding of their circumstances

Lurking - Hiding true intentions while gathering information to use against others

Lying - Giving into temptation to deliberately deceive others with false information

Malice - Harboring ill will and desire to harm others in heart and mind

Manipulation - Using emotional tactics to control others' decisions for personal benefit

Meddling - Interfering in others' affairs without invitation or legitimate authority

Misunderstanding - Careless communication or assumptions that demons exploit to twist others' intentions and create conflicts

Mockery - Giving in to temptation to make fun of others to embarrass and belittle them

Murder - Taking another's life or systematically destroying their reputation and spirit

Narcissistic behavior - Deep insecurity or sense of entitlement that demons use to destroy empathy in a person by causing them to have an obsessive self-centered focus

People-pleasing - Fear of rejection that demons exploit into manipulating others by telling them only what they want to hear

Persecuting - Systematically harming others for their beliefs or characteristics

Pretension - Insecurity that demons mask through acting false and phony to impress or deceive others

Provoking - Stirring up anger and conflict in others for personal advantage or entertainment

Rage – Anger or frustration that demons amplify beyond healthy limits into expressions that terrify and harm others

Rebellion - Giving in to temptation to reject legitimate authority and encourage others to do the same

Revenge - Seeking to harm others in return for perceived wrongs rather than trusting God to give fair justice or mercy in repentance

Selfishness – When demons amplify normal self-interest into caring only for one's own needs while ignoring others

Slander - Spreading false and damaging information about others to harm their reputation

Stealing - Taking what belongs to others without permission for personal gain

Strife - Creating ongoing conflict and tension in relationships rather than pursuing peace

Unloving behavior - Treating others rudely, or without empathy or kindness

Unmerciful behavior – Feeling entitled in refusing to show grace and forgiveness to others

Untrustworthy behavior - Breaking promises and betraying others' confidence for personal advantage

Verbal abuse - Using words as weapons to harm and control others emotionally and mentally

Violence - Using physical force to harm and intimidate others to get one's way

Whisperers - Spreading secrets and rumors in ways that damage relationships and trust

Wickedness - Actively choosing to harm others through evil actions and intentions

4: Sexual Abuse

Adultery - Sexual unfaithfulness that breaks marriage vows and destroys trust

Fornication - Engaging in sexual activity outside the commitment and protection of marriage

Lewdness - Displaying sexuality in crude and inappropriate ways that degrade intimacy

Lust of the flesh - Being controlled by physical desires rather than subordinating them to the higher desires of the Holy Spirit

Lustful eyes - Looking at others as sexual objects rather than people with dignity and worth

Masturbation - Using sexuality for selfish lust rather than the shared intimacy and connection of marriage

Obscenity - Using sexual themes to degrade and corrupt rather than honor the gift of intimacy

Pornography - Consuming sexual imagery that perverts physical desires and objectifies people

Destructive passion - Allowing sexual feelings to override wisdom, morality, and respect for others

Promiscuity - Having multiple sexual partners without the commitment and love that protects intimacy

Sensuality - Making physical pleasure the highest priority in life above love and spiritual growth

Sex addiction - Using sexuality compulsively to cope with emotional problems rather than seeking healing

Sexual immorality - Any sexual behavior that violates God's design for intimacy within marriage commitment

The Battle Is Ours Through Christ

Demons know that when we claim the blood of Jesus to set us free, their right to attach or occupy is broken. The demons will do their best to convince us that nothing changed, that we're just as weak as before we prayed the prayer. They hope that we will surrender to and trust in sin again so they can regain their right of attachment.

But Paul made it clear that everything has changed when we claim the blood of Jesus: "I can do all things through Christ who strengthens me" (Philippians 4:13). Praise God, He has not left us alone to fight the battle against demons.

In fact, Paul writes that God wants His strength and His victory to be ours: "Be strong in the Lord, and in the power of His might. Put on the whole armor of God, that you may be able to stand against the wiles of the devil. For we do not wrestle against flesh and blood, but against principalities, against powers, against the rulers of the darkness of this age, against spiritual ... wickedness" (Ephesians 6:10-18).

When We Fail, We're Not Forgotten

One of my favorite Christian authors wrote something that gave me great hope: "There are those who have known the pardoning love of Christ and who really desire to be children of God, yet they realize that their character is imperfect, their life faulty, and they are ready to doubt whether their hearts have been renewed by the Holy Spirit. To such I would say, Do not draw back in despair. We shall often have to bow down and weep at the feet of Jesus because of our shortcomings and mistakes, but we are not to be discouraged" (Ellen G. White, *Steps to Christ*, p. 64).

She continues: "Even if we are overcome by the enemy, we are not cast off, not forsaken and rejected of God. No; Christ is at the right hand of God, who also maketh intercession for us. The beloved John wrote, 'These things write I unto you, that ye sin not. And if any man sin, we have an advocate with the Father, Jesus Christ the righteous' (1 John 2:1). And do not forget the words of Christ, 'The Father Himself loveth you' (John 16:27). He desires to restore you to Himself, to see His own purity and holiness reflected in you" (ibid., p. 64).

Here's the beautiful promise: "If you will but yield yourself to Him, He that hath begun a good work in you will carry it forward to the day of Jesus Christ. Pray more fervently; believe more fully. As we come to distrust our own power, let us trust the power of our Redeemer, and we shall praise Him who is the health of our countenance" (ibid., p. 64).

And here's something encouraging: "The closer you come to Jesus, the more faulty you will appear in your own eyes; for your vision will be clearer, and your imperfections will be seen in broad and distinct contrast to His perfect nature. This is evidence that Satan's delusions have lost their power; that the vivifying influence of the Spirit of God is arousing you" (ibid., p. 64).

Our Call to Victory

We no longer need to be satisfied to be "not too sinful." Instead, we can unite our lives with Jesus in sinless living by His strength. This is the path the 144,000 spoken of in Revelation have chosen: "These are the ones who follow the Lamb wherever He goes.... And in their mouth was found no deceit: for they are without fault before the throne of God" (Revelation 14:4–5).

Join me in making a daily commitment to die to self and to be without fault before the throne of God, a place demons cannot go.

The Bible says, "In [God's] presence is fullness of joy; at [His] right hand there are pleasures forevermore" (Psalm 16:11). Ask God to change your likes and dislikes, and your desires will be deeply satisfied with new and wonderful experiences and joys. God will show us the true path to abundant life.

The Bible tells us to "put off your old self, which is being corrupted by its deceitful desires; to be made new in the attitude of your minds; and to put on the new self, created to be like God in true righteousness and holiness" (Ephesians 4:22-24, NIV).

This is the victory that Jesus died to give us. This is the freedom that His blood purchased. This is the character that God wants to develop in each of us. Will you claim it today?

EPILOGUE:

When a Christian dons the armor of God and engages in battle against the rulers of darkness in this world, there will inevitably be fallout, which can be painful. King David faced this reality as well. In the Old Testament we read about David's experience; he described it in these words:

> The Lord is my rock and my fortress and my deliverer; the God of my strength, in whom I will trust; my shield and the horn of my salvation, my stronghold and my refuge; my Savior, You save me from violence. I will call upon the Lord, who is worthy to be praised; So shall I be saved from my enemies.

> When the waves of death surrounded me, the floods of ungodliness made me afraid. The sorrows of Sheol surrounded me; the snares of death confronted me. In my distress I called upon the Lord, and cried out to my God; He heard my voice from His temple, and my cry entered His ears.

> Then the earth shook and trembled; the foundations of heaven quaked and were shaken, because He was angry. Smoke went up from His nostrils, and devouring fire from His mouth; coals were kindled by it. He bowed the heavens also, and came down with darkness under His feet. He rode upon a cherub, and flew; and He was seen upon the wings of the wind. He made darkness canopies around Him, dark waters and thick clouds of the skies. From the brightness before Him coals of fire were kindled.

> The Lord thundered from heaven, and the Most High uttered His voice. He sent out arrows and scattered them; lightning bolts, and He vanquished them. Then the channels of the sea were seen, the foundations of the world were uncovered, at the rebuke of the Lord, at the blast of the breath of His nostrils.

He sent from above, He took me, He drew me out of many waters. He delivered me from my strong enemy, from those who hated me; for they were too strong for me. They confronted me in the day of my calamity, but the Lord was my support. He also brought me out into a broad place; He delivered me because He delighted in me.

The Lord rewarded me according to my righteousness; according to the cleanness of my hands He has recompensed me. (2 Samuel 22:2-21)

While God served as David's shield and protector, David noted that God drew him out of many waters, delivered him from his strong enemy, and rescued him in times of calamity.

As warriors for Christ, we should not assume that our faith and endurance will go untested. I have experienced severe tests since I was interviewed on a YouTube podcast with Little Light Studios in July 2024 titled *I Cast Demons Out of People*. In the first six months after its release, over 160 individuals worldwide have contacted me for help to escape demonic attacks. The devil and his demons are not pleased that my life is devoted "to open their eyes, in order to turn them from darkness to light, and from the power of Satan to God" (Acts 26:18).

Use this QR code to view the 2024 Little Light Studios interview. Note that a second interview is planned on the same channel in the summer of 2025.

In October 2024 while I was touring Europe to speak on mission and spiritual warfare, my wife Wendy, home in Cambodia, fell seriously ill with pneumonia. After the pneumonia cleared, she was diagnosed with stage four kidney failure and chronic lung disease, accompanied by very low hemoglobin. She was so ill that I feared for her life.

I sat down with my Bible and asked God where He wanted me to read. I heard the still, small voice of the Holy Spirit direct me to Ezekiel 24. There I encountered these words: "Also the word of the Lord came to me, saying, son of man, behold, I take away from you the desire of your eyes with one stroke; yet you shall neither mourn nor weep, nor shall your tears run down" (Ezekiel 24:15, 16).

I paused, took a deep breath, and began a conversation with God that went something like this: "Father, are you trying to tell me that today you are going to take my wife of forty-two years from me?" (I paused, struggling to hold back the tears Ezekiel was told not to cry). "Father, you know what is eternally best. If this is your will, I give you permission to do what is right, but I can't promise that I won't cry."

I surrendered Wendy to God, placing the decision of whether she lived or died in His hands. The first thing I did the next morning was check to see whether Wendy had survived the night. She had, and I thanked God.

Perhaps I did not hear God instruct me to read from Ezekiel that morning, and maybe my mind just chose that chapter by chance. However, I believe that in this cosmic battle, God wanted to demonstrate to Satan that I was ready to surrender everything to serve Him. I am grateful that God helped me pass that test.

At this writing five months later, Wendy is improving but continues to suffer from chronic kidney disease, chronic lung disease, and low hemoglobin. I see this as an attack from Satan to hinder our work. But the testing was soon to intensify.

But the testing was soon to intensify.

In January 2025, two weeks after I began writing this book, my five-year-old grandson Mikey, who lived next door, was tragically killed in an accident. His father and a group of students were digging around the base of a termite mound. Their goal was to topple this two-meter (6.5 feet) tall mass. After several hours of work, they had no reason to expect it would fall immediately.

My grandson, playing nearby, had been warned to stay away from the work area. Suddenly, he approached the termite mound and squatted down under the area that had been dug out. In an instant, the mound collapsed on him, crushing his head and breaking his leg. My son rushed him to the hospital, where they managed to revive his heart, but he was later diagnosed as brain dead.

Everyone loved Mikey. Thousands of people worldwide prayed for him. It would not be a difficult task for God to restore Mikey's brain and body functions. I prayed that God would do what was eternally best. After five days, his parents made the heart-wrenching decision to discontinue life support, leaving Mikey fully in God's hands.

We buried Mikey the following day.

I believe it was no coincidence that the termite mound collapsed just as Mikey was squatting beneath it. This incident feels like another demonic attack on our family, aimed at discouraging me from engaging in spiritual warfare and, specifically, from writing this book.

We miss Mikey dearly, but knowing that five-year-old Mikey loved the Lord gives us comfort; we believe his name is written in the Book of Life. We will soon be reunited with him, this time for eternity. While the demons may have orchestrated Mikey's death, they can do nothing to prevent his resurrection when Jesus returns.

As for me and Mikey's dad, we are more determined than ever to partner with God in rescuing as many souls as possible from the clutches of Satan. Our new motto is "Salvation of the lost at any cost."

Each day, I strive to die to self and allow Jesus to live through me. Jesus said, "If you have seen me, you have seen the Father" (John 14:9, CEV). I want people to see the Father through me, too. I take heart in the promise of Jesus: "I am the vine, you are the branches. He who abides in Me, and I in him, bears much fruit; for without me you can do nothing" (John 15:5).

May my life and yours produce much fruit for the Kingdom of God.